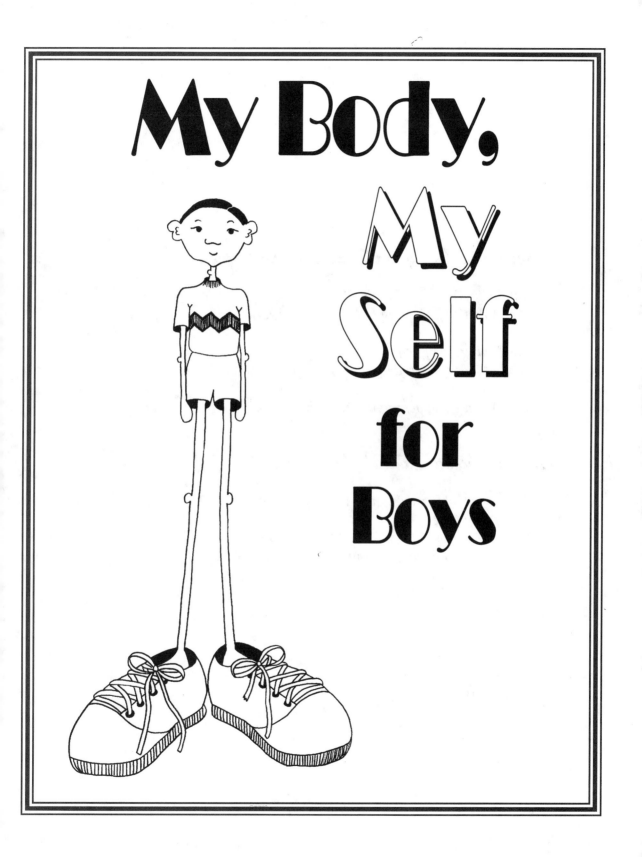

My Body, My Self for Boys

Other books by Lynda Madaras and Area Madaras

My Body, My Self for Girls:
The "What's Happening to My Body?" Workbook

My Feelings, My Self:
Lynda Madaras' Growing-Up Guide for Girls

The "What's Happening to My Body?" Book for Girls

Other books by Lynda Madaras

The "What's Happening to My Body?" Book for Boys

Lynda Madaras Talks to Teens About AIDS:
An Essential Guide for Parents, Teachers and Young People

My Body, My Self

for Boys

The "What's Happening to My Body?" Workbook

Lynda Madaras and Area Madaras

NEWMARKET PRESS

NEW YORK

Dedication

For our fathers, who aren't in heaven.

96 97 98 99   10 9 8 7 6 5 4 3 2 1

Library of Congress Cataloging-in-Publication Data

Madaras, Lynda.
My body, my self for boys / Lynda Madaras and Area Madaras.
p.   cm.
"The companion workbook to The what's happening to my body? book for boys."
Summary: Explanatory text and workbook exercises present information about such
aspects of male puberty as penis size, masturbation, and acne.
ISBN 1–55704–230–6 (pbk.)
1. Teenage boys—Growth—Juvenile literature.   2. Teenage boys—Physiology—Juvenile
literature.   3. Puberty—Juvenile literature.   4. Sex instruction for boys—Juvenile literature.
[1. Puberty.   2. Teenage boys.   3. Sex instruction for boys.]   I. Madaras, Area.   II. Madaras,
Lynda.   What's happening to my body? book for boys.   III. Title.
RJ143.M327   1995   95–40401
613'.04233—dc20   CIP
                                                                                                                      AC

Quantity Purchases:
Companies, professional groups, clubs, and other organizations may qualify for special terms
when ordering quantities of this title. For information, write Special Sales, Newmarket Press,
18 East 48th Street, New York, NY 10017, or call (212) 832-3575 or (800) 726-0600.

Cover design by Tania Garcia
Illustrations by Lisa Hales

MANUFACTURED IN THE UNITED STATES OF AMERICA

Contents

Acknowledgments

We'd like to thank all the men and boys who made this book possible by sharing their feelings and experiences with us. Thanks to Andrew F., Chico F., Michael F., Moshe F., Victor F., Jonathan K., Michael L., Andy M., George M., John O., Warren O., Tracy R., Larry S., Everett T., Big Al V., Bill V., the boys in our classes and workshops, and the many boys and men who have written to us over the years.

Preface

Hi, we're Lynda and Area Madaras.

We're the mother and daughter team who put this book together (with a lot of help from our friends). We've been writing books and teaching classes on puberty and sexuality for years. Some years ago, Lynda and a young friend wrote another book called *The "What's Happening to My Body?" Book for Boys* that explained the physical and emotional changes a boy goes through during his preteen and teen years, as his body changes from a child's into a man's body. This time of change is known as puberty, and the book explained how and why puberty happens and answered the many questions that have come up in our sexuality education classes over the years. We received thousands of letters from boys all over the world with new questions and experiences to share, and that's how this book came about.

This book is a companion to the earlier book for boys, though you don't need *The "What's Happening to My Body?" Book* to use this one. This book covers many of the same topics covered in the earlier book, though not in as much detail. The big difference between the two books is that this is a workbook, with exercises, quizzes, and other activities that will help you learn about the changes that take place in your body during puberty.

Like the first book, this book owes a great deal to the many boys and girls who have been students in our classes over the years and to the families who have attended our puberty and sexuality workshops. Much of the material in this book was developed and refined with their help. Indeed, without their kind patience when exercises and activities didn't work out as planned and their enthusiasm when they did, this book would not have been written. We also owe a big thanks to the many men and boys who have written to us over the years, and to those who spoke with us personally while we wrote the book.

We hope you (and the friends and family members you'll recruit for some of the activities) enjoy the activities and exercises for the book and that it will answer some of the questions you'll have as you enter this new stage of your life.

Lynda Madaras and Area Madaras
October 1995

PART ONE

WHAT'S HAPPENING TO YOU?

Imagine that it's late on a dark, stormy night. All is quiet as you stare out your bedroom window into the darkness.

Suddenly, the storm clouds part. Moonlight floods your bedroom, striking your mirror. You turn to look at yourself and come face to face with the truth. There's no longer any doubt about it. Your body is definitely changing!

Perhaps the first change you noticed was the coarser, darker hair growing on your arms and legs and in places where it never grew before. By now, hair may even be growing on your face.

You may have noticed the whole shape of your body changing—broader, wider shoulders; thicker, more powerful muscles. You may be growing at an amazing rate. Your feet may seem too big and your arms too long.

Your forehead is becoming higher and your jaw longer and lower, so that it juts out more. Your body may have a new, unfamiliar odor. And you may be experiencing new and intense feelings and urges.

WHAT'S HAPPENING TO YOU?

A. YOU'RE TURNING INTO A WEREWOLF.

B. YOU'RE GOING THROUGH PUBERTY.

Answer: ⇨⇨⇨⇨⇨⇨⇨⇨⇨

Puberty Is the Answer

You're not turning into a werewolf; you're turning into a man! Puberty is the time in a boy's life when his body develops from a child's body into a man's body.

Luckily, puberty doesn't happen overnight, and it's nowhere near as scary as turning into a werewolf. Still, puberty does mean lots of change, and it helps to know ahead of time what to expect. That's where this book comes in. It explains how, when, and why your body changes.

But this is not just a book about puberty; it's also a book about you. It is filled with exercises, activities, and places to record what's happening to you. In fact, by the time you're through, this book will be not only *about* you, it will be *by* you as well!

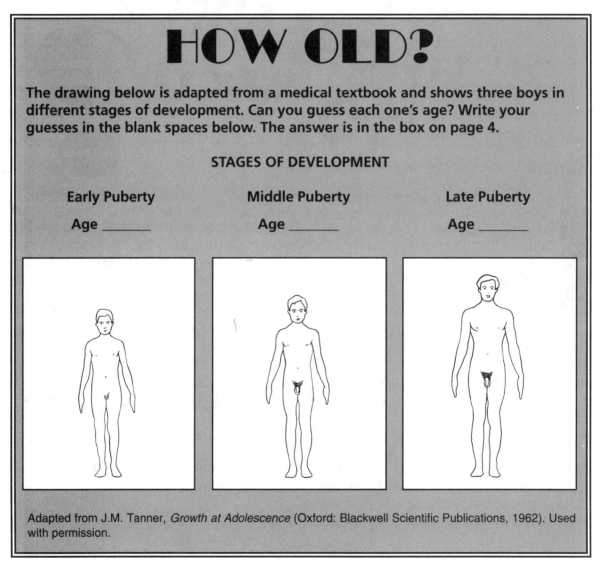

HOW OLD?

The drawing below is adapted from a medical textbook and shows three boys in different stages of development. Can you guess each one's age? Write your guesses in the blank spaces below. The answer is in the box on page 4.

STAGES OF DEVELOPMENT

Early Puberty

Age _____

Middle Puberty

Age _____

Late Puberty

Age _____

Adapted from J.M. Tanner, *Growth at Adolescence* (Oxford: Blackwell Scientific Publications, 1962). Used with permission.

PUBERTY CHANGES

● Hair is more oily; you may need to wash it more often.

● Skin is more oily; you may have problems with pimples.

● Nipples enlarge, darken in color, and may be tender or sore.

● Breasts may swell and may remain enlarged for a year or two.

● Sex organs grow and develop.

● Curly pubic hair grows on and around sex organs.

● Muscles are thicker and more developed, and body strength increases.

● Hair on legs increases and may darken in color.

● Feet enlarge and perspire more; foot odor may be a problem.

● You go through a growth spurt and your weight and height increase rapidly. You grow taller faster than ever before. Your feet grow first. Your arms and legs grow before the trunk of your body grows.

● Hair grows on upper lip and on cheeks.

● Shoulders are wider and broader.

● Underarm hair grows; you may notice more perspiration (sweat) and body odor.

● Hair may grow on chest, back, shoulders, or elsewhere.

● Hair on arms may increase and darken in color.

● Erections (when the penis gets stiff and hard for a while) happen more often.

● And during puberty, for the first time, a boy ejaculates—releases a teaspoon or so of a white, creamy fluid called semen from the opening in the tip of the penis. You'll learn all about ejaculation and these other changes as you do the exercises in this book.

3

Starting Lineup

Puberty changes don't happen all at once. First you notice one change, then another, then another. Often these changes happen in the order shown in the chart below; that is, first, the testicles and scrotum enlarge; second, pubic hairs appear; and so on down the list.

But things don't always happen in this exact order. You may find that the changes happen to you in a somewhat different order.

Use the chart below to keep a record of the order in which these changes happen to you. When you first notice one of the changes on the chart, put a 1 next to it. When you notice the second, put a 2 in the blank space next to that change, and so on, until you've filled in all the blank spaces in the *You* column of the chart.

If you've already noticed some of these changes, you can start filling out the chart now. (If you can't remember the exact order, just make your best guess.)

YOU	TYPICAL ORDER OF PUBERTY CHANGES
	1. Testicles and scrotum grow larger
	2. First pubic hair
	3. Penis enlarges
	4. Ejaculation (release of semen)
	5. Height growth spurt
	6. Shoulders broaden
	7. Voice changes
	8. Hair on upper lip or underarms

Your Life: Past, Present, & Future

Since this book is about you, let's look at your life. What's it like now? How is it different from the way it was in the past or will be in the future? Filling in the chart below will help you think about these questions.

	Past	Present	Future
The way I spend most of my time			
The people I'm closest to			
My favorite thing to do			
The most important thing in my life			

Thoughts & Feelings: Growing Up

It was great. I remember thinking, "I'm not a kid anymore!" I loved it!
—John, age 26

It took too long. I was a late bloomer. It was a relief when it finally happened.
—Miles, age 21

I was angry and embarrassed and scared. Nobody told me what was going on.
—Terry, age 18

I was sort of confused because I didn't understand what was happening. It was kind of scary.
—Paul, age 34

It was neat; it was cool. Sort of like "the arrival."
—Joseph, age 20

People make it sound like it's this big dramatic thing that all of a sudden happens one day. It's not like that. It's not like some guy pops up and says, "Hey, kid, this is it. Now it's going to happen to you."
—Jackson, age 33

I don't really think about it. I just sorta go with the flow.
—Christian, age 9

It's like one minute it was really cool and the next minute I was totally freaked out about it.
—Zack, age 17

WHAT ABOUT YOU?

You've heard what these boys and men had to say; now it's your turn. On the next page, you'll find a racewriting exercise with space for you to write what you think. To find out how to racewrite, check out the instructions below.

Just write whatever comes into your head! It doesn't necessarily have to make sense, and you don't have to worry about spelling and punctuation. (Don't you wish your English class was this easy?) The key to racewriting is that you time yourself, and the only rule is that once you start writing, you can't stop until you reach the end of the page. Then check out how long it took you, and write the time in the watch at the bottom of the page.

If you get stuck, don't know how you feel, can't think of anything to say, write just that—"I'm stuck," or "I can't think of anything to say." Write it over and over again as long as you have to, just so long as you keep writing without stopping until you've filled all the blank space. Now no cheating by writing too big! The idea here is to get as many thoughts down as fast as you can. Good luck!

Racewriting

What are your feelings about growing up and the way your body is—or soon will be—changing? Are you excited, scared, or both? How far along are you? Do you wish you were further along? How do you feel about the changes you've noticed so far? Are you looking forward to the changes to come, or would you rather just forget the whole thing?

If you're already well into puberty, do you remember what you felt like before? Do you feel different now? What questions do you still have? What are you feeling right now?

Remember to write as fast as you can, and don't stop for anything! Get your watch ready so you can fill in your time at the end. Ready, set, GO!

_____

_____

_____

_____

_____

_____

_____

_____

_____

write your time here

ASKING QUESTIONS... FINDING ANSWERS

If you're like most boys, you probably have a lot of questions about puberty. Sometimes it's hard to ask questions about your body because people act like you should already know it all. But that's silly. No one "just knows" things; we learn from other people. So having questions is perfectly natural. We hope this book will answer some of these questions and help you learn the facts in a way that's fun and entertaining.

We won't pretend that this book will answer all your questions. For one thing, it's an exercise book more than an information/facts book. We have written an information/facts book about puberty, and it's listed, along with similar books, in Resource Section (see page 93).

No book, no matter how good, can answer all your questions. Fortunately, there is a solution close at hand. To find out what it is, solve the riddle in the box below.

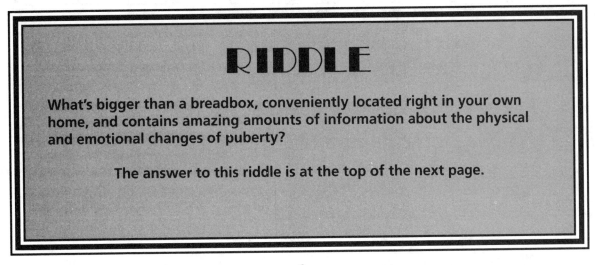

RIDDLE

What's bigger than a breadbox, conveniently located right in your own home, and contains amazing amounts of information about the physical and emotional changes of puberty?

The answer to this riddle is at the top of the next page.

THE ANSWER:
Your Mom, Your Dad,
or Whatever Adult(s) You Live With

These folks are the answer. They're the most logical ones to turn to when you have questions, need advice, or just want to talk about what's happening to you. They can understand what you're going through; after all, they've been through it, too!

What if you're ready and willing, but your parents are too chicken to talk?

Or maybe you're the one who's all red in the face, too shy and embarrassed to talk.

If you've had these sorts of problems, you're not alone. Take a look at the next page.

All Kinds of Families

You may live with one or both of your birth parents or with adoptive, foster, or stepparent(s). Or you may live with one or more of your grandparents, other relatives, or family friends. You name it! There are all kinds of families. If the words we've used in the next few exercises (or elsewhere in this book) don't apply to your family living situation, just substitute ones that do.

It'd be easier to talk to them if they were close to my age.

—Tom, age 17

I get a little embarrassed.

—Chad, age 17

Parents don't want to talk about it.

—Peter, age 13

I wish they'd just bring it up first.

—Adam, age 14

I'm afraid of asking stupid questions. People think I should know.

—Andy, age 12

I feel like I need an interpreter!

—Gene, age 14

I wish they'd talk about when they grew up.

—Michael, age 11

They've never brought it up, so I s'pose it'd be all right if we did talk.

—Jamie, age 10

Easier Said Than Done?

As the boys quoted above point out, talking to your parents isn't always the easiest thing in the world. If you have problems talking to your parents (or even if you don't), try the exercises on the next few pages. They'll help you bring up the subject and help your parents remember what it was like to go through puberty. They'll also help you get past the embarrassment that so often keeps parents and kids from talking about these things.

Remember When...

Explain to your parent(s) that you need their help with one of your workbook exercises. Then have them answer the questions below.

INTERVIEW I: When you were my age...

What was your favorite radio or TV show?_____

What kind of music did you listen to?_____

Who was your best friend?_____

What did you most enjoy doing?_____

What did you want to be when you grew up?_____

Where did you go to school?_____

Did they teach puberty or sex education in your school?_____

Did your parents talk to you about puberty and how babies are made?_____

Do you wish they'd talked to you more?_____

INTERVIEW II: When you were going through puberty...

Did you start to develop earlier, later, or about the same time as your friends?_____

What were the first changes you noticed, and how old were you?_____

_____

_____

How did you feel about these changes?_____

_____

What did your parents tell you about puberty and how babies are made? _____

_____

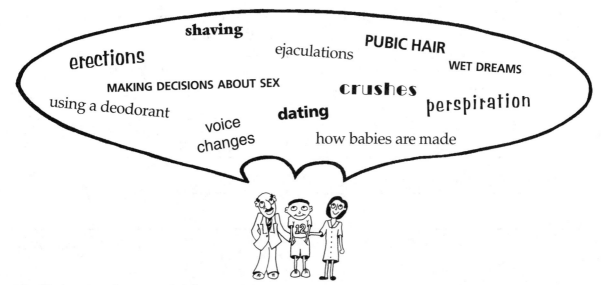

shaving

ejaculations

PUBIC HAIR

erections

WET DREAMS

MAKING DECISIONS ABOUT SEX

crushes

using a deodorant

perspiration

dating

voice changes

how babies are made

Talking About Puberty

In the conversation balloon above, we've listed some of the topics that parents and sons might talk about during the puberty years. Can you think of any others?

Part I: For the first part of the exercise, you and a parent will take turns filling in the empty balloon below. You go first.

In the balloon, write a puberty topic that parents and sons might want to discuss. Then pass the book to your parent and have him or her write one. Continue taking turns until you've either filled up the entire space (in which case you're both winners) or until one of you can't think of another topic (in which case the last person to make an entry is the winner). When you've finished, go on to the next page.

Part II: Look at the two conversation balloons on page 13 and pick the three topics that would be most embarrassing or hardest for you to discuss with your parent. Write the three topics in the spaces below.

Then cover up your answers, and have your parent list the three topics that she/he would find most embarrassing or hardest to discuss with you.

1. _____

2. _____

3. _____

1. _____

2. _____

3. _____

Part III: Now compare your lists, answering the questions and following the instructions below.

❑ Do the same or similar topics appear on both of your lists? Put a check mark in front of those items.

❑ Other than the items that are the same on both lists, are there topics on the other person's list that you too would find difficult or embarrassing to discuss? If so, mark those items with check marks too.

❑ Are there any topics on your lists that are so embarrassing that it would be very difficult or impossible to discuss? Put a star in front of those items.

Almost all parents and sons have at least some degree of embarrassment about one topic or another, which can make it difficult to talk about these things. But by doing this exercise, you should

have a clearer idea of just where you may run into difficulties. You may even find that simply doing this exercise and identifying the embarrassment have already made it easier to talk about these things!

Below are some other suggestions you may find useful. Read and discuss each suggestion, putting an ✗ in front of those that might work for you.

❑ Have a third person (a doctor, nurse, or counselor) talk with both of you about the topic.

❑ Read books or pamphlets, or watch videos about the topic together and talk about it (see Resource Section, page 93).

❑ Have your parent read a book or talk to another person and then share the information with you.

❑ Find another person (family member, nurse, doctor) to talk to you.

PART TWO

THE MALE SEX ORGANS: An Owner's Manual

The sex organs are also known as the *reproductive organs* because they are the parts of our bodies that make us able to re-produce—that is, to make babies. These organs are also called the *genital organs* or *genitals*. We have these organs on both the inside and the outside of our bodies. *External* means "outside." So you probably won't be surprised to learn that the sex organs on the outside of our bod-ies are called the *external sex organs*. They are also called the *external reproductive organs* or *external genital organs*.

In this section, you'll learn about the external male sex organs: the *penis* and *scrotum* (the pouch of skin that lies below and behind the penis). You'll also learn a bit about the *testicles*, two organs that lie within the scrotum.

By the time you've finished this chap-ter, you'll know what these organs look like, how they work, and how they change during puberty. You'll even be able to figure out how far along in puberty you are!

Circumcised or Not?

Circumcision is an operation in which the *foreskin*, a fold of skin around the top of the penis, is removed. Most males in this country have been circumcised, but some haven't.

If you've been circumcised, you probably don't remember the operation because it's usually done when a male baby is only a few days old. Older children and grown men rarely have their penises circumcised.

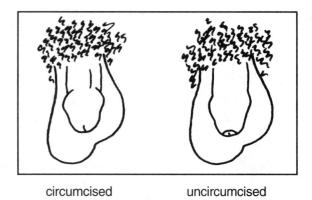

circumcised   uncircumcised

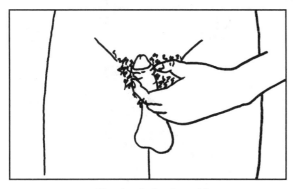

pulling back the foreskin

Some parents (Jewish and Muslim parents, for instance) have their male babies circumcised for religious reasons. Some have it done because doctors say it makes it easier to keep the penis clean.

Uncircumcised males should gently pull the foreskin back and clean under it so they don't develop problems with odor or infection. Otherwise, there's no difference between circumcised and uncircumcised males. Except for the foreskin, their penises look, feel, and work the same way.

Have You Been Circumcised?

If you have been, your penis won't have a foreskin that can be pulled back to uncover the head of the penis. If you're unsure, ask your parents. In fact, even if you are sure, you might ask them why they decided to (or not to) have you circumcised. If you were circumcised for religious reasons, you might ask when and where it was done, who was there, and how loudly you howled. Use the space below to note what you learn.

_____

_____

_____

_____

The Male Sex Organs

If you take a few moments to color in the different body parts, you'll remember them better. These are important parts of the body, so it's worth the effort. Just follow the instructions below.

P.S. The instructions call for a red and a blue pencil, but any two colors will do.

◆ Find the *shaft,* or *body,* of the penis and color it red.

◆ Next, find the *glans,* or *head,* of the penis and color it with red and blue stripes.

◆ The ring, or ridge, of tissue that circles the lower edge of the glans is called the *corona.** Color it blue.

◆ At the tip of the penis is the small *urinary opening,* through which urine (pee) leaves the body. Circle it in blue.

◆ Use your red pencil to shade in the coarse, curly *pubic hair.*

◆ Behind and below the penis is a pouch, or bag, of skin called the *scrotum* (or *scrotal sac*) that holds two egg-shaped organs called the *testicles.* You can't see testicles in this drawing, but find the scrotum and color it with red and blue polka dots.

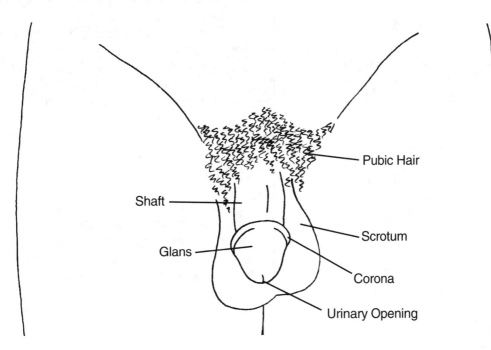

Shaft

Glans

Pubic Hair

Scrotum

Corona

Urinary Opening

*Note that you can see the glans and the corona because this is a drawing of a circumcised penis. If it were a drawing of an uncircumcised penis, these parts would be covered by the foreskin.

Having an Erection

When the penis gets long and hard and sticks out from the body at an angle, you're having an *erection*. *Boner* is a slang word for an erection; and when it's erect, the penis can feel so hard that it seems as if there really is a bone in there. But there isn't.

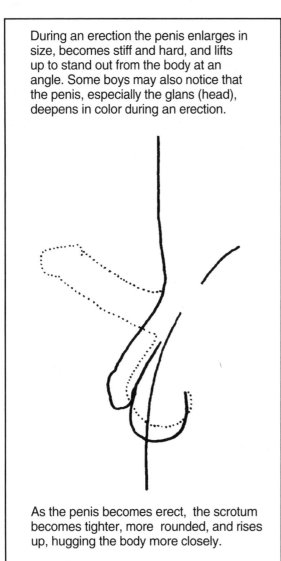

During an erection the penis enlarges in size, becomes stiff and hard, and lifts up to stand out from the body at an angle. Some boys may also notice that the penis, especially the glans (head), deepens in color during an erection.

As the penis becomes erect, the scrotum becomes tighter, more rounded, and rises up, hugging the body more closely.

No Bones About It!

There are no bones inside the penis, just lots of soft, spongy tissue. During an erection, this spongy tissue fills with blood. The veins that carry blood to the penis dilate (open wider), increasing the blood flow. The spongy tissues swell up and become stiff with blood, which causes the penis to grow larger and become so stiff and hard that it rises up and sticks out from the body at an angle—and bingo, you've got an erection!

An erection can develop slowly or within a matter of a few seconds. Once erect, the penis can stay that way for some time, or the erection may disappear as quickly as it came. It all depends on the situation. Sooner or later, though, the veins constrict (become narrow) again. The extra blood that was in the penis is drawn back into the bloodstream, and the penis becomes soft and floppy again.

Men and boys and even little babies have erections. Often, they happen while you sleep, and one may still be there to greet you when you wake. You can have one when the penis is touched, when you're feeling "sexy" or having "sexy" thoughts, or when you're nervous or excited. Sometimes, especially during puberty, they happen for no particular reason.

Depending on where you are when it happens, having an erection for no reason at all can be kind of embarrassing. Check out the box on the next page to work on some ideas for how to cope with this if it happens to you.

How Do You Cope?

Having an erection when you don't want to can be *sooooo* embarrassing. What are some things you can do to cope with this problem? Write your suggestions in the space below. Then turn the page and compare your advice to the advice we heard from other guys.

_____

_____

_____

_____

What's Your Angle?

An erect penis may stick out at various angles, or it may stand nearly straight up. When erect, the penis may be straight or it may curve to the right, to the left, or some other way. No matter what your angle is, it's perfectly normal!

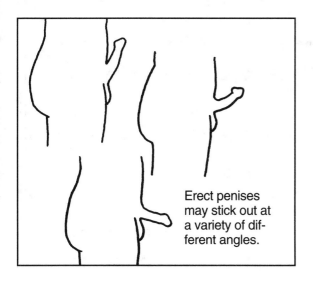

Erect penises may stick out at a variety of different angles.

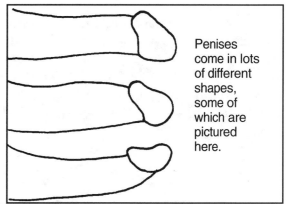

Penises come in lots of different shapes, some of which are pictured here.

Shapes and Sizes

You may have seen pictures of penises (like the ones in this book) and been worried if yours doesn't look just like that. But penises come in many different shapes and sizes. Still, it's easy to get concerned if you're not sure what's normal and what's not. Here's the basic rule: Anything goes. Some penises are long; some are short. Some are fat, and some are skinny. And they're all perfectly normal!

The BIG Question:
Is Mine Too Small?

Surveys show that most men either think their penises are too small or at least wish theirs were larger. In the letters we get from male readers, the most common questions and concerns are about penis size. So if you've worried or wondered about penis size, you're not alone. We hope the facts below will satisfy your curiosity and lay your worries to rest.

The LONG and short of It

For starters, you should know that the size of your penis has nothing to do with how macho, brave, or attractive you are. It has nothing to do with what kind of lover, husband, or father you'll be. Your penis size is a reflection of one and only one thing: the size of your penis.

About Average

There's a lot of disagreement among the experts about what's average. In general, though, the adult male penis is roughly 3 to 4 inches long when soft and roughly 6 inches long when erect. The shorter-when-soft ones grow more when they become erect, so they all end up being about the same size when erect. But don't get all flustered if your measurements don't match these numbers. For one thing, you're still growing. For another, you may not be measuring as far down the penis as they do. Besides, as you well know, your penis changes size, and not just during erections, either. Being afraid, cold, or nervous reduces the blood inside the penis, making it smaller in size. If you've ever waded into cold water, you know what we mean! Being relaxed or warm increases the blood in the penis, making it larger. And the stiffness and size of your erection also varies. So it's hard to say what the average size of one man's penis is, much less the average of all men.

To Cope with Erections You Could:

- wear baggy pants and long shirts if they keep happening
- shift your notebook to cover it or carry a book to hold in front of your erection
- sit down when you get an erection
- put your hands in your pockets to try and hide it
- tie a sweatshirt around your waist and let the sleeves cover it
- try to focus on something else until it goes away
- just remember that it's probably more noticeable to you than to anyone else

Penis Enlargers

You've probably seen the ads. You know the ones—they try to make you feel like your penis isn't large enough just so you'll buy their product. Don't be taken in. These products aren't only stupid and pointless—they're also dangerous.

We've received countless letters from boys who have tried these products and were disappointed, to say the least. Basically, the kits contain weights you attach to the penis or scrotum. This doesn't really make the penis larger, but it can do permanent damage by stretching out the skin and tissue. In our opinion, calling these penis enlargers is $sTRETCHING$ the truth.

OWNER'S MANUAL:
Routine Care and Maintenance of the Genitals

EQUIPMENT:
● Washcloth and soap.

MAINTENANCE SCHEDULE:
● Clean at least once every 24 hours.
● On the uncircumcised model, the foreskin should be pulled back to ensure thorough cleaning.
● Apply clean underwear daily.
● For best results, do not use unclean athletic supporters as this can lead to fungus buildup. (See "jock itch" in the Troubleshooting Guide on page 22.)

Injury Prevention

EQUIPMENT:
● Jockstrap (athletic supporter)

PURPOSE:
● To protect the testicles and penis while you're doing athletic activities.

TYPES:
● Some fit like briefs; others are held on with straps (hence the name *jockstrap*).
● The soft-cup type holds the genitals snugly against the body so they don't get knocked around (though some guys feel that regular briefs do the job well enough).
● The hard-cup type provides extra protection for sports where you risk taking a blow to the groin. They are required by some schools and athletic programs.

SIZING:
● Measure your waist! That's all you need to know to buy an athletic supporter because the size has nothing to do with penis or testicle size. The cup will fit you no matter what size your genitals are, so all you need is your waist size.
● Adult sizes start in the 26-to-32-inch waist range; youth sizes start at 20 inches.

BUYING:
● If you know your waist size ahead of time, they're easy to buy. Just find your waist size and you're set! You don't even have to try it on!
● Jockstraps are sold in sporting goods stores and departments and in the first-aid aisle of some drugstores.

Medical Alert

SUDDEN, SEVERE TESTICLE PAIN:
● *Following Accident or Other Injury:* Pain may be severe, but it usually does not require medical treatment.
    However, if pain doesn't begin to let up within an hour or so, if it worsens, or if there's bruising or swelling, see your doctor or go to an emergency room immediately.
● *Without Accident or Injury:* See your doctor or go to an emergency room immediately, even if the pain goes away as suddenly as it appeared.

Troubleshooting Guide

JOCK ITCH:
● Dirty underwear or a sweaty jockstrap stuffed in a gym locker can be a breeding ground for a fungus infection that causes a scaly, itchy rash in the genital area. It can usually be treated with antifungals such as Tinactin, which can be purchased without a prescription. If the problem persists, see your doctor.

FORESKIN PROBLEMS:
● In uncircumcised males, the foreskin may be so tight or adherent (stuck) that it can't be pulled back over the head of the penis. This is not a common problem. But if it happens to you, don't try to force the foreskin to retract; you could damage the tissues. Instead, see your doctor.

Testicle Size

The drawing you see here shows an *orchidometer*, a string of wooden or plastic ovals of different size that doctors use to measure testicles. The numbers on the ovals of the orchidometer show their size in measurements called *milliliters (ml)*. By comparing your testicles to the ovals of the orchidometer, a doctor can make a good estimate of their size.

Measurements of testicle size are useful in determining whether or not a boy has started puberty, how far along he is in his development, how much further he has to go, and when he'll develop into a fully mature, adult male. These measurements will also be used in some of the exercises in the following pages. The box below will tell you how to size your testicles.

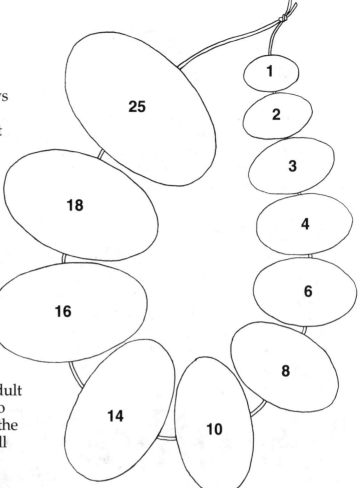

Sizing Your Testicles

We couldn't include an actual orchidometer with this book, but we did manage to fit in a life-sized drawing you can use to size your testicles.

First size one testicle and then the other (and don't worry if one is larger than the other; it's perfectly normal). You can size the testicle using one or both hands. You might want to hold the testicle up against the drawing, or you can stand in front of a mirror, book in one hand, testicle in the other. Do whatever helps you to decide which of the various ovals of the orchidometer is closest to your testicle in size. Then fill in the blank spaces below.

Today's date: _____   Right testicle: _____ml   Left testicle: _____ml

STAGES OF GROWTH & DEVELOPMENT

One of the biggest changes in puberty is that your sex organs mature. Doctors have divided this growth and development into the five stages described in the boxes below and on the following pages.

Ages & Stages

In describing the five stages, we've tried to give you a rough idea of how old a boy is likely to be as he reaches each new stage. But as you know, we each have our own timetable when it comes to puberty. In the descriptions that follow, we've given the average ages at which boys reach each stage. However, few people are exactly average, and there's a great deal of variation from boy to boy in when a particular stage will start and how long it will last. So we've given you not only the average age and average amount of time spent in each stage, but also a range of ages and times. That means we've given you the earliest and the latest ages at which boys are likely to start each stage, as well as the least amount of time and the most amount of time boys are likely to be in each stage. It's important to note, though, that these are just typical times and that some perfectly normal boys will start earlier or later than the ranges we've given.

Once you've read through these stages, try to figure out which stage you're closest to. Put a check mark in the box next to that stage.

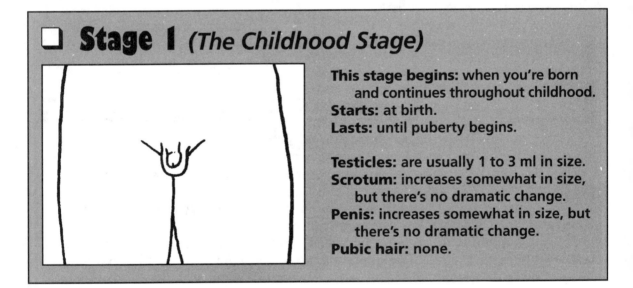

☐ Stage 1 (The Childhood Stage)

This stage begins: when you're born and continues throughout childhood.
Starts: at birth.
Lasts: until puberty begins.

Testicles: are usually 1 to 3 ml in size.
Scrotum: increases somewhat in size, but there's no dramatic change.
Penis: increases somewhat in size, but there's no dramatic change.
Pubic hair: none.

Stage 2 *(The Beginning of Puberty)*

This stage begins: when your testicles start growing noticeably larger.
Starts: average is 11 to 12 years old; range is 9 to 16 years old.
Lasts: average is about 13 months; range is 5 to 26 months.

Testicles: have usually reached at least 4 ml in size and are at least 1 inch long. As development continues, one testicle hangs lower than the other (otherwise they'd knock together when you walk).
Scrotum: has also enlarged and hangs lower. The skin of the scrotum is thinner and not as smooth as it was in Stage 1. It's also reddish in color, though in dark-skinned boys this may appear as a deepening in color rather than redness.
Penis: may grow slightly larger, but basically there's little or no change.
Pubic hair: may appear in this stage or not until Stage 3 or later (see below). The first hairs are long and slightly curly and grow at the base of the penis and scrotum.

Stage 3 *(The Lengthening Stage)*

This stage begins: when your penis starts growing noticeably longer.
Starts: average is 13 to 14 years old; range is 10 to 15 years old.
Lasts: average is about 10 months; range is 2 to 19 months.

Testicles: continue to enlarge. They're usually 7 to 16 ml in this stage.
Scrotum: continues to develop as it did in Stage 2.
Penis: may have grown a bit wider, but the biggest increase is in length.
Pubic hair: usually makes its first appearance in this stage. It may be sparse at first. As development continues, it darkens, becomes curlier, and covers a wider area.

☐ Stage 4 *(The Widening Stage)*

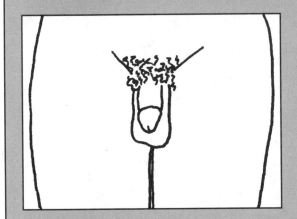

This stage begins: when your penis starts growing noticeably.
Starts: average is 14 to 15 years old; range is 11 to 17 years old.
Lasts: average is about 24 months; range is 5 to 36 months.

Testicles: are usually about 12 to 24 ml in size and about 1½ inches long.
Scrotum: continues developing as in earlier stages and skin darkens.
Penis: is a bit longer and quite a bit wider and the glans (head) is more distinct.
Pubic hair: has usually developed by the time a boy reaches this stage; however, as many as 15 percent of boys in this stage are without pubic hair. Once it has appeared, pubic hair continues to get curlier and eventually darkens in color and forms an upside-down triangle pattern. As development continues, it will spread beyond this triangle pattern and may grow up toward the belly, out onto the thighs, or elsewhere in the genital area.

☐ Stage 5 *(The Adult Stage)*

This stage begins: when your sex organs are fully developed.
Starts: average is 16 years old; range is 14 to 18 years old.
Lasts: the rest of your life.

Testicles: are fully developed at 16 to 27 ml in size and about 1¾ inches long.
Scrotum: is fully developed and deeper in color.
Penis: is fully developed and deeper in color.
Pubic hair: is fairly well developed but may continue to grow until about age 20.

The Growth and Development of My Favorite Person

Use these pages to keep a record of your development. Every 3 to 6 months fill in another box. You might need to refer back to the descriptions of the different stages, which begin on page 24, or to page 23, which shows the orchidometer used to measure testicle size.

Today's Date: _____   Puberty Stage: _____

Testicle Size: (right) _____ ml   (left) _____ ml

Changes I've noticed lately: _____

_____

_____

Today's Date: _____   Puberty Stage: _____

Testicle Size: (right) _____ ml   (left) _____ ml

Changes I've noticed lately: _____

_____

_____

Today's Date: _____   Puberty Stage: _____

Testicle Size: (right) _____ ml   (left) _____ ml

Changes I've noticed lately: _____

_____

_____

Today's Date: _____   Puberty Stage: _____

Testicle Size: (right) _____ ml   (left) _____ ml

Changes I've noticed lately: _____

_____

_____

Today's Date: _____   Puberty Stage: _____

Testicle Size: (right) _____ ml   (left) _____ ml

Changes I've noticed lately: _____

_____

_____

Today's Date: _____   Puberty Stage: _____

Testicle Size: (right) _____ ml   (left) _____ ml

Changes I've noticed lately: _____

_____

_____

Today's Date: _____   Puberty Stage: _____

Testicle Size: (right) _____ ml   (left) _____ ml

Changes I've noticed lately: _____

_____

_____

Today's Date: _____   Puberty Stage: _____

Testicle Size: (right) _____ ml   (left) _____ ml

Changes I've noticed lately: _____

_____

_____

Today's Date: _____   Puberty Stage: _____

Testicle Size: (right) _____ ml   (left) _____ ml

Changes I've noticed lately: _____

_____

_____

Today's Date: _____   Puberty Stage: _____

Testicle Size: (right) _____ ml   (left) _____ ml

Changes I've noticed lately: _____

_____

_____

Today's Date: _____   Puberty Stage: _____

Testicle Size: (right) _____ ml   (left) _____ ml

Changes I've noticed lately: _____

_____

_____

How Much Longer?

Every boy is different, and no one can tell for sure how long it will take before you reach the adult stage, but the chart below will help you make a good guess.

Column I lists the stages, and Column II gives the average amount of time it takes to get from the beginning of that stage to the beginning of the next one. But few boys are exactly average, and the timing of these stages varies quite a bit. So Column III gives a range of times.

EXAMPLE: Looking down Column I to Stage 3 and across to Column II, we see that the average time for Stage 3 is 10 months. Moving across to Column III, we learn that most boys (94 percent) will take somewhere between 2 and 19 months to get through Stage 3. (The other 6 percent will take more or less time than this.)

To estimate how long it will take you to get to Stage 5 and be finished with puberty, complete Parts I and II.

Part I

Step A. Find your current stage in Column I and read across the chart to Column II to find the average amount of time boys spend in this stage. Write

the number of months in the square here.

Step B. Estimate how many months you've been in this stage. Write the number here.

Step C. Subtract the number in the circle from the one in the box. Write the answer here.

Part II

If you're currently in Stage 4 of development: Copy the number in the triangle into the star below.

If you're currently in Stage 3: Add 24 to the number in the triangle and write the total in the star below.

If you're currently in Stage 2: Add 34 to the number in the triangle and write the total in the star below.

This is the estimated number of months it will take you to reach Stage 5.

REMEMBER: This is only an estimate based on averages; it may take you more or less time than this. But we promise you this: You will get there!

Column I Stage	Column II The Average Time	Column III 94 Out of 100 Boys Will Take Between . . .
2	About 13 months	5 to 26 months
3	About 10 months	2 to 19 months
4	About 24 months	5 to 36 months

Test Your I.Q.

With This P.Q.

(puberty quiz)

True	False		
___	___	**1.**	A boy who starts puberty at an early age will reach the adult stage sooner than a boy who starts to develop later.
___	___	**2.**	If a guy finds loose pubic hairs on his sheets, pajamas, or underclothes, he should see a doctor.
___	___	**3.**	Pubic hair is always the same color as the hair on your head.
___	___	**4.**	If you haven't shown any signs of puberty by age 15, you should see a doctor.
___	___	**5.**	Plucking your pubic hairs will keep them from growing.
___	___	**6.**	The amount of pubic hair a man has depends on his racial, ethnic, and family background.
___	___	**7.**	It's normal for the testicles to grow before the penis.
___	___	**8.**	In earlier stages of puberty, the glans isn't as developed as it is in later stages.
___	___	**9.**	Sometimes the testicles are closer to the body than at other times.
___	___	**10.**	In adult males, the left testicle usually hangs lower than the right one.

Turn to the next page to see how you did!

ANSWERS

· ·

1. **False.** How early or late a boy starts to develop doesn't have anything to do with how fast he develops.

2. **False.** Just like the hair on your head, it's normal for pubic hairs to shed and be replaced by new hairs.

3. **False.** Pubic hair may be the same color as the hair on your head, or it may be lighter or darker. When you become an old man, your pubic hair may turn gray, just like the hair on your head.

4. **True.** There are many perfectly normal, healthy boys who don't go through puberty until they're 15 or older. But boys whose sex organs have not begun to develop by age 15 should see a doctor to make sure there isn't a problem.

5. **False.** If you pluck your pubic hairs, they'll just grow back. Besides, plucking these hairs hurts and could also cause an infection.

6. **True.** Men from certain racial and ethnic groups tend to have more pubic hair than men from other groups. A man's personal family background (what he inherits from his parents) determines how much pubic hair he has.

7. **True.** Testicles begin to grow at the start of puberty, and the penis usually starts to grow about a year later.

8. **True.** The glans becomes more noticeable in Stage 4.

9. **True.** When it's cold, the scrotum draws the testicles closer to the body to keep them warm. When it's warm, the scrotum hangs lower, allowing the testicles to cool off.

10. **True.** One testicle hangs lower than the other so you can walk without crunching them together. In 85 percent of men, it's the left testicle that hangs lower. But it's perfectly normal for the right one to hang lower instead.

There's Another Name For It

Use the space below to make a quick list of other names you've heard for the penis, scrotum, or testicles. Your list can include scientific or medical terms, baby words, and slang words, even so-called "dirty" words. (After all, this is your own private book.)

_____

_____

_____

_____

_____

_____

You're No Dumb Elbow!

Chances are nobody's ever called you a dumb elbow, and we doubt that you've ever lost your temper and called someone a stupid foot. But take a look at the list you just made and think of all the names—both proper and improper ones—for the male sex organs. Then think of the insults and name-calling you've heard. We bet you've heard the names for the sexual parts of the body used as insults.

Why do you think people use sexual words to insult others? Use the space below to jot down your ideas about this. Then ask your friends and family the same question and compare their answers with yours.

_____

_____

_____

_____

_____

_____

_____

_____

You Said It!

This will help you to pronounce words that may be new to you.

circumcised (sir-come-SIZED)
circumcision (sir-come-SI-zhun)
corona (ko-RO-na)
erection (e-REK-shun)
glans (GLANZ)

genitals (JEN-a-tuls)
orchidometer (OR-ki-DOM-e-ter)
penis (PEE-niss)
puberty (PEW-bur-tee)
pubic (PEW-bic)
scrotum (SKROH-tum)
testes (TES-teez)
testicles (TES-ti-kuls)
urinary (YUR-in-airee)

PUBERTY DISASTERS

Everybody has a puberty disaster story to tell. If it didn't happen to them, it happened to somebody they knew or to somebody who knew somebody they knew. Our friend Brian told us this one.

In 8th grade, at the end of gym class one day the big, macho football coach growls,

"OK. YOU GUYS, ALL OF YOU BRING IN YOUR NUT CUPS TOMORROW."

So the next day, everybody shows up with their jockstraps. Except for one kid. He brings in his mama's nut dish, you know, her special nut dish she sets out when company comes.

Needless to say, he never lived it down.

Trading Disasters

If you have a story better than our friend Brian's, use that. Otherwise, use Brian's story. What you're going to do is this: You're going to make a bet with your dad, your grandpa, big brother, or some other man in your life, someone you like or look up to.

You set the terms of the bet (loser pays for the popcorn at the movies, has to eat a can of dog food, give up his life savings—whatever). The bet is this: You tell him Brian's story, and he has a week to come up with a better one. If he does (be fair now), you lose. But you can take his story and go bet somebody else. Eventually, you're bound to win. When you do, write the winning disaster story in the space below.

_____

_____

_____

_____

_____

_____

_____

_____

_____

_____

PART 3
THE INSIDE STORY

In Part 2, we talked about the external male sex organs—the ones on the outside of the body— and how they grow and develop during puberty. Before these changes on the outside of your body even begin to happen, other changes are already taking place on the inside.

Internal means "inside"; and here in Part 3, we'll focus on the internal sex organs—the ones inside your body. Like the external sex organs, the internal sex organs grow and develop during puberty. In the following pages, you'll learn how these organs change during these years.

Both the internal and external sex organs are also known as the *reproductive organs*, and together they make up your *reproductive system*. *Re* means "to do again" and *produce* means "to make," so *reproduce* means "to make again."

You may be wondering "to make what again?" The answer is simple: It's you and me! Reproductive systems are what allow human beings to make more human beings—-that is, to make babies. Of course, you're not ready to be a father yet, and won't be for some time, but during puberty your body is getting ready for the time in your life when you may decide to start a family.

What Happened on Your Birth Day?

Since we're talking about reproduction, let's talk about the day you were produced—your birth day! We don't mean the day you eat ice cream and cake and celebrate being another year older. That's your birthday. We're talking about your birth day—the day you were born!

Get ready to do an interview. Depending on your family situation, you might interview one or both of your natural, adoptive, or foster parents; your grandparents; or whatever adult(s) you live with. We've listed some sample questions. Adapt them to suit your family situation. For instance, if your adoptive parents weren't at your birth, you can ask about when they first saw you. And add some questions of your own.

Sample Questions

1. Where was I born (city, hospital, etc.)? At what time was I born?

2. Did I take a long time to come, or was I born quickly?

3. What was the weather like on the day I was born?

4. Who else was there that day (family, friends, medical persons, etc.)?

5. How much did I weigh? How many inches long was I?

6. What did I look like?

7. How was my name chosen?

8. Did anything unusual or funny happen when I was born?

9. Can you tell me what else you remember about the day I was born?

The most interesting thing I heard about my birth day was:

_____

_____

_____

_____

_____

_____

_____

EXTRA, EXTRA, Read All About It!

Now that you have an idea of what happened in your world on your birth day, what about the rest of the world? Your arrival was undoubtedly the biggest thing that happened to your parents that day. But you probably didn't make the front page of the paper. Who did? What was the headline story in the paper on your birth day?

A trip to the library will answer your question. Ask the librarian to help you find out the headline news on the day you were born. You can look at local, regional, and national newspapers in the library's collection of back issues. You might ask if *Time, Newsweek, Rolling Stone,* or any other magazine had an issue that came out the same day you did.

Make a birthday present for yourself. Photocopy one of the front pages or magazine covers published on your birth day and frame it!

Puberty Begins in the Brain

Long before you notice any of the changes of puberty, a part of your brain called the *pituitary gland* begins making increasing amounts of certain hormones. *Hormones* are chemicals made in one part of the body that travel through the bloodstream to other parts of the body to tell the body how to behave.

Your body produces all sorts of hormones. The pituitary alone produces so many hormones with such long names that we'd bore you to death if we tried to list them all. Instead, we'll just tell you that certain pituitary hormones travel through the bloodstream to the testicles, causing them to begin making a hormone of their own. This hormone is called *testosterone,* and it plays an important role in growth and development during puberty.

◯ Puberty starts in the brain. Around the age of 8 or 9, the pituitary gland, which is located at the base of the brain, begins to make larger amounts of certain hormones.

◯ The hormones from the pituitary gland in the brain are released into the bloodstream and travel to the testicles. The pituitary hormones cause the testicles to begin making testosterone.

◯ Testosterone travels to the other parts of the body and plays a role in many of the changes that happen during puberty, including the development of the sex organs, the puberty growth spurt, deepening of the voice, growth of pubic hair and other body hair, and muscular development. Testosterone also plays a role in the development of sperm.

Sperm

During puberty, the testicles not only make increasing amounts of testosterone, but they also produce sperm for the first time. *Sperm* are the male *seeds,* or reproductive cells. When joined with a female reproductive cell (called an *ovum*), a baby can grow.

Sperm are so tiny you'd need a microscope to see them, but they look something like tadpoles.

Ejaculation

During puberty a boy also ejaculates (releases sperm from his body) for the first time. Sperm begin to develop in the testicles and are stored in coiled tubes attached to the top of each testicle. When a male is about to ejaculate, the mature sperm travel up into the body through a series of tubes where they mix with various fluids. This mixture, known as *semen,* then travels through a tube in the center of the penis and spurts out the opening in the tip of the penis during ejaculation. In all, about 1 teaspoon or so of white, creamy semen is ejaculated. We'll talk about ejaculation in more detail in a bit. But first, try the coloring exercise on the next page to familiarize yourself with the internal male sex organs.

Amazing Sperm Facts

★ A boy begins making sperm in his testicles during puberty and continues to do so throughout most of his life.

★ The testicles have to be slightly cooler than normal body temperature to produce healthy sperm. So when it's cold outside, the scrotum pulls them closer to the body to keep them warm; when it's warm, the scrotum hangs lower so they stay cool.

★ A normal ejaculation contains 150 to 500 million sperm.

★ If you laid 500 sperm in a line end to end, the line would only be 1 inch long.

★ The average male makes about 10 to 30 billion sperm a month.

★ You can't run out of sperm, and you can't use them up because your body is always making more.

★ It takes about 2 1/2 to 3 months from the time sperm start to develop in the testicles until they've passed through the epididymis and are ready to leave the body.

The Internal Reproductive Organs

Below is a simplified drawing of the male reproductive organs from the side view. If you take a few minutes to color in the various parts, you'll be able to remember what's what. These are important parts of the body, so it's worth the effort. Just follow the instructions below.

P.S. The instructions call for a red and a blue pencil, but any two colors will do.

A. **Testicles** — place where sperm are made and testosterone is produced. Since this is a side view, you can see only one of the testicles. Color it red.

B. **Epididymis** — long, coiled tubes attached to the upper, rear portion of each testicle. Sperm mature here. Color the epididymis seen in this drawing with blue polka dots.

C. **Vas deferens** (or just plain vas) — set of narrow tubes through which sperm travel as they move up into the body. Each vas runs from the epi-didymis (**B**), up into the body, and loops around the bladder (**D**). At the base of the bladder, it is joined by a tube from the seminal vesicle (**E**) and then enters the prostate (**F**), where it connects to the urethra (**G**). Color the vas shown in this side view blue.

D. **Bladder** — place where urine (pee) is stored. It's not part of the reproductive system, but color it with blue stripes.

E. **Seminal vesicles** — place where sticky fluid is made that is added to sperm and other fluids to make semen. Color the seminal vesicle seen in this side view with red stripes.

F. **Prostate gland** — gland that adds more fluid to the semen. Color it with red polka dots.

G. **Urethra** — hollow tube in the center of the penis. Both semen and urine leave the body through this tube (but never at the same time! See the box on page 41). Color the urethra red.

H. **Urinary, or urethral, opening** — external opening at the end of the urethra, located in the center of the glans (head) of the penis. Circle it with blue.

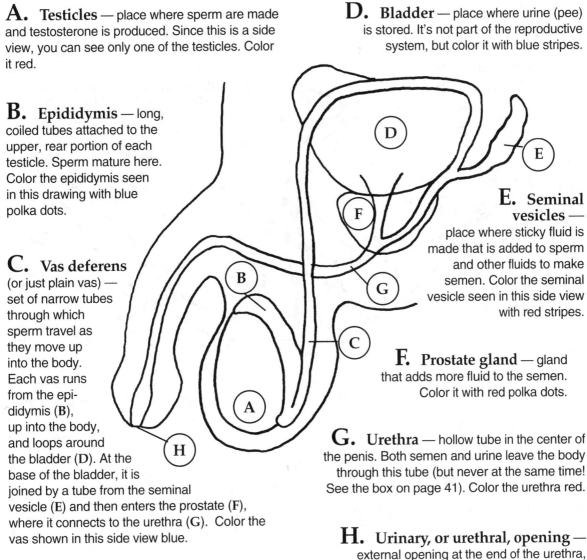

Ejaculation: The Inside Story

Now that you have an idea of what the different parts of the internal reproductive system look like and how they connect to one another, let's look at what happens on the inside during ejaculation.

The drawing below shows what happens shortly before and during ejaculation. As you can see, the penis is erect—that is, stiff and hard. (Remember we talked about erections in Part 2.) Not all erections end in ejaculations, but all ejaculations begin with an erection.

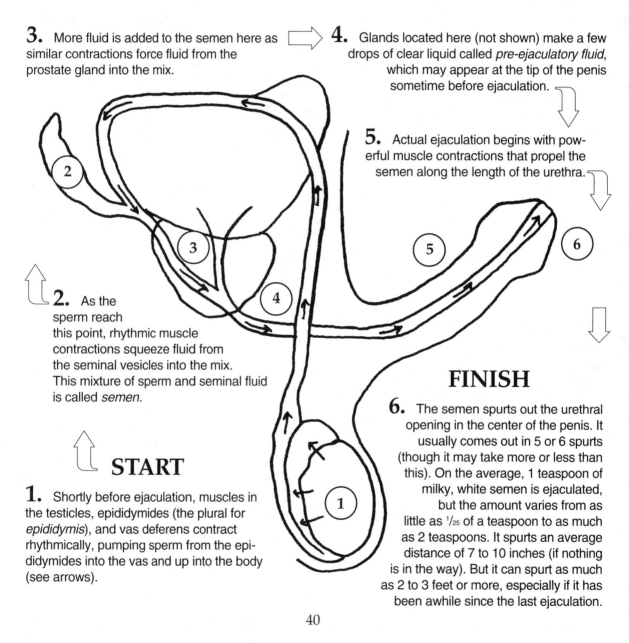

3. More fluid is added to the semen here as similar contractions force fluid from the prostate gland into the mix.

4. Glands located here (not shown) make a few drops of clear liquid called *pre-ejaculatory fluid*, which may appear at the tip of the penis sometime before ejaculation.

5. Actual ejaculation begins with powerful muscle contractions that propel the semen along the length of the urethra.

2. As the sperm reach this point, rhythmic muscle contractions squeeze fluid from the seminal vesicles into the mix. This mixture of sperm and seminal fluid is called *semen*.

START

1. Shortly before ejaculation, muscles in the testicles, epididymides (the plural for *epididymis*), and vas deferens contract rhythmically, pumping sperm from the epididymides into the vas and up into the body (see arrows).

FINISH

6. The semen spurts out the urethral opening in the center of the penis. It usually comes out in 5 or 6 spurts (though it may take more or less than this). On the average, 1 teaspoon of milky, white semen is ejaculated, but the amount varies from as little as $1/25$ of a teaspoon to as much as 2 teaspoons. It spurts an average distance of 7 to 10 inches (if nothing is in the way). But it can spurt as much as 2 to 3 feet or more, especially if it has been awhile since the last ejaculation.

Orgasm

When a male ejaculates, he usually has the intense, pleasurable feeling that is known as *orgasm*. It's difficult to explain exactly how an orgasm feels. Some people compare it to a sneeze because both involve convulsive spasms of muscle contractions. But having an orgasm is much more pleasurable than sneezing. Perhaps a better explanation is that an orgasm is an intense spasm or waves of pleasure that begin in the sex organs and radiate outward, sometimes involving the whole body. The intensity of an orgasm may vary from one ejaculation to the next, but most people agree that it's a pretty good feeling.

In addition to the changes described on the previous page, several other things happen before and during orgasm and ejaculation.

- The scrotum tightens, and muscle contractions pull the testicles closer to the body.

- The opening in the tip of the penis becomes more slit-like, and the head may become a deeper or more purplish-red color.

- The skin on the stomach, chest, neck, and face may get flushed or reddish in color. This is called the *sex flush*, and it happens in 1 out of every 4 males.

- The nipples may become erect and deeper in color.

- The heart rate and breathing will become more rapid.

- There may be muscle contractions in arms, legs, stomach, and/or feet.

- The body may sweat, especially the hands and feet.

After ejaculation and orgasm, the body returns to its normal state. This may happen fairly quickly or rather slowly. The penis becomes soft again and gradually returns to its normal size. Men usually feel relaxed and may feel sleepy after orgasm.

Some men are able to have another ejaculation and orgasm almost right away. Usually, though, there's a period of time that must pass—anywhere from a few minutes to a half hour, several hours, or a day or so—before a man is able to get another erection and is ready to have another orgasm.

Can You Urinate and Ejaculate at the Same Time?

Because urine (pee) and semen both leave the body through the same tube, boys often wonder if it's possible for urine and semen to get mixed together. It's a logical question, but the answer is no. Urine and semen can't travel through the urethra at the same time. When a male is about to ejaculate, a special valve closes, preventing urine from leaving the bladder. So, it's just not possible to ejaculate and urinate at the same time.

First Ejaculation—When?

The age at which a boy has his first ejaculation varies quite a bit. The average age for the first ejaculation is around 13 to 14 years old. Nine out of ten boys (90 percent of boys) will have their first ejaculation between the ages of 11 and 15 years, but one out of every ten boys (10 percent of boys) will be older than age 15 or younger than age 11 when he first ejaculates.

First Ejaculation—How?

Most boys have their first ejaculation as a result of masturbation or having a wet dream.

Wet Dreams

About ⅓ of boys have their first ejaculation while they are asleep. This is called a *nocturnal emission*, or *wet dream*. Wet dreams can happen to older males, but they're more common among boys going through puberty.

It's called a wet dream because your bed or pajamas may be slightly wet from the semen ejaculated and many boys remember having a "sexy" dream when they awaken. However, other boys don't recall having a sexy dream, and some don't recall having a dream of any kind.

It's possible for a boy to have wet dreams without knowing it. He may not wake up right after the dream and there's really very little semen, so it may dry up, leaving only a slight water mark that may go unnoticed. But not all boys have wet dreams. It's normal if you do and normal if you don't.

The word *nocturnal* refers to nighttime. Actually, though, a wet dream could happen anytime you're asleep—if you took a nap during the day, for example. But you do have to be asleep. When you're awake, you might have a spontaneous erection (when the penis gets hard for no particular reason), but there's no such thing as spontaneous ejaculations, ones that happen for no reason at all. When you're awake, ejaculations happen for a reason,

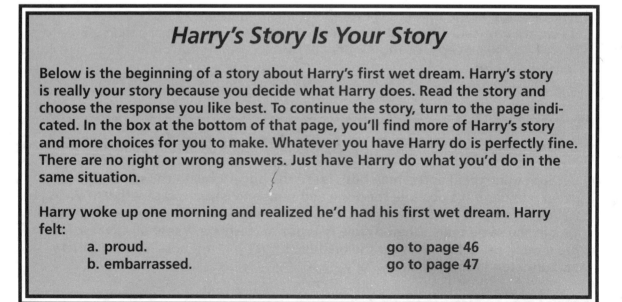

Harry's Story Is Your Story

Below is the beginning of a story about Harry's first wet dream. Harry's story is really your story because you decide what Harry does. Read the story and choose the response you like best. To continue the story, turn to the page indicated. In the box at the bottom of that page, you'll find more of Harry's story and more choices for you to make. Whatever you have Harry do is perfectly fine. There are no right or wrong answers. Just have Harry do what you'd do in the same situation.

Harry woke up one morning and realized he'd had his first wet dream. Harry felt:

    a. proud.   **go to page 46**
    b. embarrassed.   **go to page 47**

and during puberty the most common reason is that a boy is masturbating.

Masturbation

About ⅔ of boys have their first ejaculation while masturbating. *Masturbation* means "deliberate touching or stroking of the sex organs."

Masturbation doesn't always cause ejaculation. But once a male has begun making sperm, he'll usually ejaculate if he continues masturbating long enough.

People used to tell all sorts of stories about masturbation—like it'll make you go blind or grow hair on the palms of your hands, or even that you'd turn into a werewolf. None of these things is true. If they were, there would be a lot of hairy-palmed, blind werewolves on the planet because the fact of the matter is that most people masturbate at some point during their lives.

If you're like the boys in our classes, you probably have a lot of questions about masturbation. Use the space below to list your questions. Then compare your questions to the list of commonly asked questions that we've answered on the next two pages.

_____

_____

_____

_____

_____

_____

_____

Commonly Asked Questions About Masturbation

1. Do most boys masturbate?

Yes, most boys (and men) masturbate. In fact, over 90 percent of men have masturbated to the point of orgasm at some point in their lives. Some start during puberty or younger, and others don't start until their older. Still others never masturbate at all. It's normal if you do, and it's normal if you don't.

2. How often do boys masturbate?

Among those who do masturbate, the average 15-year-old male masturbates about twice a week. Some boys masturbate several times a day; some once or twice a day; some once or twice a week. Some boys masturbate less often than this, and some never masturbate.

3. What if you masturbate too much?

Unless it interferes with your normal activities (like going to school, doing homework or chores, or hanging out with friends and family), there really is no such thing as "too much." Your body sets its own limits. If it gets tired, you just won't be able to get an erection until your body has rested. If you masturbate a lot, you might find that your penis gets sore from all the rubbing; but it's not serious, and it'll be fine after you let it rest for a while. The fact is that masturbation isn't physically harmful in any way.

4. If you masturbate a lot, will you run out of sperm?

No, you can't run out of sperm. As we explained earlier, your body is constantly making millions of new sperm each day. There's just no way you could run out.

5. Is it normal to imagine things when you masturbate?

Sure, this is called *having a sexual fantasy,* and it's completely normal. Sometimes people fantasize about things they'd actually like to do; other times people fantasize about things that they'd be embarrassed or feel bad about if they actually did. Again, this is perfectly normal. Some people worry that their sexual fantasies are weird or that there's something wrong with them. But we can pretty much guarantee you that no matter what fantasy you've had, there are plenty of people who have had almost the exact same fantasy. However, if your fantasies are violent and you're worried about this, you should talk to a counselor.

6. Can masturbation affect your athletic performance?

There's really no evidence that masturbation helps or hurts your athletic ability. Some athletic coaches think it's a good idea for boys to masturbate before a big game because masturbation can be a good way of relieving tension and relaxing. Other coaches tell their teams not to masturbate because they think athletes perform better when they're a little tense. If you're an athlete, you pretty much have to decide for yourself.

7. Is masturbation sinful or morally wrong?

People have very different ideas about what's morally wrong and what isn't. Today, most people do not think masturbation is morally wrong or sinful, and personally, we go along with that point of view. In the past, many religions held that masturbation was a sin; and although many religious leaders no longer feel this way, some still do. But even if a religion's official point of view is that masturbation is morally wrong, that doesn't mean that all the people in that religion, or even all the religious leaders in that religion, agree. It's sort of an individual thing, something you'll have to decide for yourself. If you're bothered by the idea that masturbation may be sinful or morally wrong, perhaps you should talk with your minister, priest, rabbi, or religious leader. Or perhaps you'll find one of the books in our resource section helpful (see page 93).

8. If you don't masturbate, what happens to all those sperm?

If sperm aren't ejaculated (like they are during masturbation or wet dreams), they are simply reabsorbed by the body.

9. How do I find out more about masturbation?

Okay, okay, we cheated here. This isn't really one of the most commonly asked questions, but we wanted to see what you had to say. Fill in your suggestions in the space below, and then turn the page to see what others have suggested.

Getting Answers To Your Questions

You could:

- 👉 look it up in a book
- 👉 talk to a doctor or nurse
- 👉 talk to your parents
- 👉 talk to an adult you know and trust
- 👉 talk to a teacher (especially a health or sex ed teacher)
- 👉 talk to a coach

You Said It!

Some of the words used in this section of the book may be new to you. The pronunciation guide below will help you to say these words correctly.

bladder (BLA-dur)
deferens (DEAF-e-renz)
ejaculate (e-JACK-you-late)
ejaculation (e-JACK-you-lay-shun)
emission (e-MISH-un)
epididymis (eh-pih-DIH-dih-mis)
hormones (HOR-moans)
masturbate (MASS-tur-bait)

masturbation (mass-tur-BAY-shun)
nocturnal (knock-TUR-nul)
orgasm (OR-gaz-um)
ovum (OH-vum)
pituitary (pih-TYOU-e-tair-ee)
prostate (PROS-tate)
reproduction (REE-proh-DUCK-shun)
reproductive (REE-proh-DUCK-tive)
semen (SEE-muhn)
seminal (SEM-ih-nul)
sperm (spurm)
testosterone (tes-TAH-stuh-rone)
urethra (you-REE-thra)
vas (vaz)
vesicles (VE-seh-kuls)

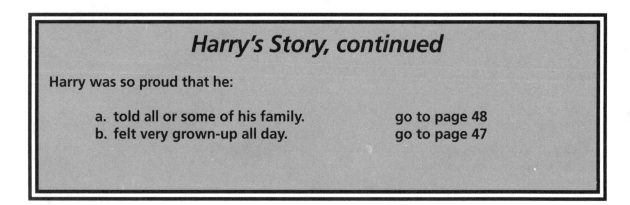

Harry's Story, continued

Harry was so proud that he:

a. told all or some of his family.　　　　go to page 48
b. felt very grown-up all day.　　　　　go to page 47

Medical Q & A

The boys in our workshops and classes sometimes have questions about medical problems that affect the internal sex organs. On this page and the next, we've included some of these questions and their answers.

What would happen if a boy had only one testicle?

Most males are born with two testicles. Every once in a while, someone is born with only one or with an undescended testicle (see the next question). Or, a testicle could be removed surgically due to disease, injury, or an accident that completely crushed the testicle.

Fortunately this sort of problem is not common. But even if this problem occurs, the reproductive system can still work normally. If a male loses one testicle, the remaining one can produce enough sperm, and he'll still be able to become a father. (Remember, a male makes millions of sperm each day.) A male's sex life is not affected by the loss of a testicle either. About the only difference a male would notice is that there's no testicle in the scrotal sac on the side of the missing testicle. Nowadays, doctors can put an *implant* made of a special material into the scrotum to make it look like there are two testicles.

What is an undescended testicle?

Before a boy is born, his testicles are up inside his body. Once he is born, they descend (come down) into his scrotal sac. Sometimes one or both testicles don't descend, and the boy has what doctors call an *undescended testicle*.

At times, cold weather, a cold bath, excitement, or extreme physical activity will cause one or both of a boy's testicles to retract, that is, to draw up close to his body for a while. But this is a temporary condition. It's not the same as an undescended testicle.

An undescended testicle is usually noticed when a male baby is born or early in life, and it sometimes corrects itself. Once in a while, the problem isn't noticed until puberty, in which case the boy must have an operation to remove the testicle. This is done because there is a greater risk of cancer developing in a testicle still undescended by the time of puberty.

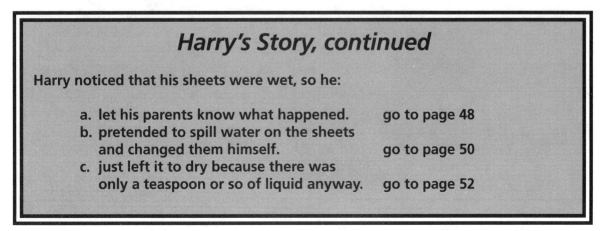

Harry's Story, continued

Harry noticed that his sheets were wet, so he:

a. let his parents know what happened.   go to page 48
b. pretended to spill water on the sheets and changed them himself.   go to page 50
c. just left it to dry because there was only a teaspoon or so of liquid anyway.   go to page 52

I was masturbating, and I didn't want to get semen all over my pajamas, so I put my finger over the top of my penis just as I was ejaculating so nothing would come out. And nothing did, but for the last couple of days I've had this pain in my penis, and this milky stuff has come out. What should I do?

Retrograde ejaculation happens when the semen is prevented from spurting out through the opening in the glans of the penis during ejaculation. In older men, there are certain medical problems that can cause retrograde ejaculation. But in boys, it usually happens as it did for the boy who asked this question.

Retrograde means "going backward." In retrograde ejaculation, the semen can't come out the end of the penis, so it's forced back down the tube in the center of the penis. It may be forced up into the bladder, which can cause the urine to be cloudy for some time. It's also possible for the semen to be forced into the prostate. Either way, there may be pain and a discharge from the penis.

In some cases, the symptoms may disappear by themselves, but if they don't, or if you have cloudy or milky urine or a dis-charge from the penis, see your doctor. You may have an infection in the prostate that needs antibiotics. (You may feel embarrassed telling the doctor, but you needn't be; doctors are used to these things.)

I have this lump in my testicle. It doesn't hurt. What is it? Is it cancer?

Though it's not common, it is possible for boys to get cancer of the testicles. When it does happen, a painless lump in the testicle can be the first symptom (see page 49 for other symptoms). But this doesn't mean that *all* lumps (or even most lumps) in the testicles are cancerous lumps. They aren't.

Many conditions can cause a painless lump in the genitals. Sometimes what feels like a lump is merely some part of the testicle—for instance, the cord that covers the vas deferens. Or the lump may actually be in the scrotum. Most of these are cysts—collections of fluid. Some cysts go away by themselves; others require an operation.

Most lumps are not cancer; but because some are, all lumps should be checked by a doctor. And you should also protect yourself by learning how to do TSE.

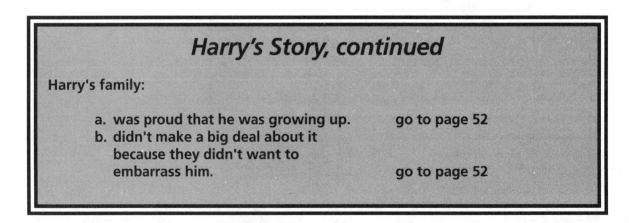

Harry's Story, continued

Harry's family:

a. was proud that he was growing up.   go to page 52
b. didn't make a big deal about it
   because they didn't want to
   embarrass him.   go to page 52

CHECK IT OUT!
Testicular Self-Exam (TSE)

What Is It?

Testicular Self-Examination (TSE) is a way of checking yourself for signs of testicular cancer. Teenagers and young men don't often get cancer, but when they do, it's likely to be testicular.

If caught early enough, testicular cancer can be completely cured. By doing TSE once a month, you have a better chance of discovering any cancer that develops while it's still in its early stages, when it's most curable. TSE only takes a few minutes a month, so it's definitely worth your time!

How Do I Do It?

It's easy! All you have to do is roll each testicle between your thumb and first three fingers until you've felt the whole surface (see Figure 1). It's a good idea to do it in the shower or bath because the warm water helps relax the scrotum.

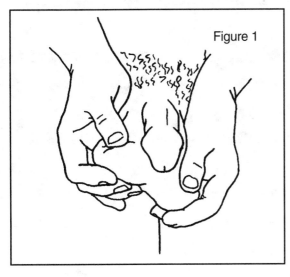

Figure 1

Remember, you're only checking the testicles, not the scrotum, epididymis, sperm tubes, or blood vessels that are also in this area (see Figure 2). Ask your doctor to show you the difference. The testicle should be egg-shaped, with a smooth surface and shape. Be on the lookout for:

- lumps
- irregularities in the shape or surface
- areas where the tissue is firmer or denser than the surrounding tissue
- pain in the testicle
- a dragging or heavy sensation

If you find any of these things or anything you think might be abnormal, go to your doctor, clinic, or medical office right away.

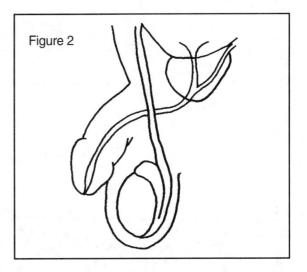

Figure 2

How Often Should I Do It?

At least once a month. Pick a regular day for doing the exam each month—the day your birthday falls on, the first day of the month, the first Sunday, whatever helps you remember to do it regularly.

Be a Lifesaver!

TSE is really easy to do, but a lot of men don't do it simply because they don't know how. Now that you know how, why not pass on the information?

Give this book to your dad or some other adult male you care about and have him sign below once he's read about testicular self-exam.

T S E

I, _____ , *do hereby certify that I have read the page on Testicular Self-Examination and promise to do my best to remain healthy by practicing Testicular Self-Examination at least once a month.*

_____
SIGNATURE

_____
DATE

Harry's Story, continued

Harry doesn't usually change his own sheets, so when his parents asked him about it he:

a. told them he had a wet dream.   go to page 48
b. just said he spilled and left it at that.   go to page 52

Invent Your Own Puberty Rite

Throughout much of human history, in culture after culture, a boy's entrance into manhood was marked by rituals, ceremonies, and customs know as *puberty rites.* Some of these puberty rites were pretty scary or dangerous—like the ones where a boy was sent out into the wilderness, unarmed and without food or water, to survive on his own for several weeks or more. When he came back—if he came back—he was considered a man.

Not all puberty rites were dangerous, though. Some involved feasting for several days and concluded with the boy sitting on a throne while everyone knelt down before him, laying presents at his feet.

Traces of puberty rites remain today in the bar mitzvah ceremony that Jewish boys go through following their thirteenth birthdays and the ceremonies still performed in some of the Native-American tribes. But for the most part, modern boys have little or nothing to mark their coming of age.

We think it's time to bring back puberty rites (not the scary ones, the fun ones). You probably won't be able to sell your parents on the throne-and-gifts-at-your-feet routine, but why not invent a puberty rite of your own?

A modern puberty rite could take many forms: a special ceremony, a camping trip with your dad, a special gift to be passed on to the next generation. It could be anything—well, anything you can get your parents to agree to.

The first thing you have to do is decide when you'll have your puberty rite. You could pick a certain date (like a birthday), a particular accomplishment, or you could celebrate after some milestone in your growth and development. For example:

- first signs of testicle growth
- first facial hair
- when your voice begins to change
- when your first pubic hair appears

Any of these events would be a good choice, or think up some of your own. Pick the three you like best and write them here.

_____

_____

_____

Next think about what kind of puberty rite you'd like. Use the space below to jot down how you might like to celebrate your transition into manhood.

_____

_____

_____

_____

_____

Now turn the page and get your parents in on the planning.

Note to Parents

Okay, parents, now it's your turn to get in on the act. We're inventing a puberty rite here, and we need your input to make your son's transition into manhood something special. First, we need an idea from you of what sort of event you'd like to use as a marker. You might choose a special birthday, or a specific pubertal change, like a changing voice, first facial hair or shave, first pubic hairs, first sign of testicle growth, or first ejaculation. Take a moment to write down three events you and your son might choose as a time for celebrating his puberty rite. You can use some of the events we've suggested, or come up with your own. Write your three choices here.

_____

_____

_____

Now think about the form your puberty rite might take. For example, you might have a special ceremony, go camp-ing, or come up with a special family gift to be passed on to future generations. Write your ideas here.

_____

_____

_____

Now all of you sit down together and compare your answers from this page and the previous one. Did you choose any of the same events? Of all the events you each came up with, which one do you think you'd like to celebrate? Write it on the first line below.

How do you want to celebrate this event? Were there any similarities in your suggestions? Now that you've seen each other's answers, talk about what you'd like to do, and outline your plans below.

_____

_____

_____

Harry's Story, conclusion

Harry still had some questions about wet dreams, so he:

    a. asked his parents.
    b. asked a teacher or school nurse.
    c. looked it up in a book (like the ones listed on page 93).

Adapted from *New Methods for Puberty Education*, Grades 4–9. Available from Planned Parenthood of Greater New Jersey, 575 Main Street, Hackensack, NJ 07601.

PART FOUR

ON YOUR MARK, GET SET, GROW!

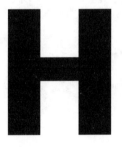

Have you begun to grow out of your shoes long before they're worn out? Are the pants you bought at the beginning of the school year already up around your ankles? If so, it may be that you've started your puberty growth spurt.

The *puberty growth spurt* is a period of especially fast growth that rapidly changes a boy's size and shape. The growth spurt affects your bones, causing them to grow at a faster rate. One result is that your height increases more rapidly than when you were younger.

Not only do you grow taller faster, but you also gain weight more rapidly during the growth spurt. At the peak of the weight spurt, it's not unusual for a boy to put on 25 or more pounds in a single year!

This increase in weight is due in part to the fact that your bones get longer and thicker and therefore weigh more. Muscle development also accounts for part of the weight gain. (And by the way, along with this increase in muscle comes an increase in strength.)

Not only does your body get taller, heavier, and stronger, but the proportions of your body (the size of certain body parts in comparison with other body parts) also change. As a result, the general contour, or shape, of your body becomes more "manly."

Even your face is affected by the puberty growth spurt. In general, a boy's face becomes longer and narrower, and its proportions change, giving you a more adult look.

A boy's appearance changes a good deal during puberty. The information and exercises in this section are designed to help you to understand how your size and shape change and to adjust to your new "looks."

Growing Up and Up and Up: The Height Spurt

Height spurt is a term for the period of time during puberty when a boy's rate of growth speeds up for a while. For most of childhood, the average boy grows taller at a rate of about 2½ inches per year. In some boys, this growth rate slows down a little just before puberty begins, so that it's actually closer to 2 inches per year. But once puberty has started and the height spurt kicks in, the growth rate begins to speed up again. It continues to increase for a while until it reaches a peak. This period of fast growth lasts only a few months before the growth rate slows down again, dropping steadily until a boy has reached his adult height around age 20 to 21. This rise and fall in the rate of growth is clearly shown in the graph you see below.

The graph is based on the average rate of growth in the so-called "average," or "typical," boy. But few of us are exactly average, and the height spurt is an individual kind of thing. When it starts, how long it lasts, and how much growth takes place can vary quite a bit from one boy to the next. So no one can tell you exactly how the puberty growth spurt will affect you. We can, however, tell you what typically happens and give you a range of ages and inches that describes what happens to most boys. (Keep in mind, though, that some perfectly normal boys —about 5 percent—will fall outside these ranges.)

The Height Spurt at a Glance

When it starts:
Average—11¾ to 13 years old
Range—10½ to 16 years old

How long it lasts:
Average—2 to 2½ years
Range—1½ to 4 years

How much you grow:
Average—8 inches
Range—4 to 12 inches

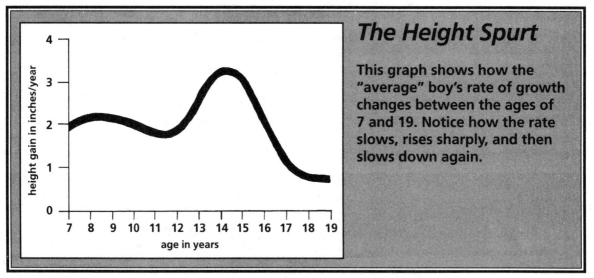

The Height Spurt

This graph shows how the "average" boy's rate of growth changes between the ages of 7 and 19. Notice how the rate slows, rises sharply, and then slows down again.

Feet First

Actually, it's feet and hands first because these are the first bones to be affected during the puberty growth spurt. Then the lower parts of the arms and legs begin their growth spurt, followed by the upper parts of these limbs. Then the spine begins to lengthen.

What does this mean to you? Well, it means that first you'll outgrow your shoes, then your pants, and finally your coats.

A Note About Measurements

Because we'll be talking a lot about height in this section, you should know how to read the abbreviations we've used here. When you see a single prime mark next to a number ('), that means the measurement is in *feet*. When you see a double prime mark ("), that means the measurement is in *inches*. So if you were to see 4'10", that would read "four feet ten inches." Get the idea?

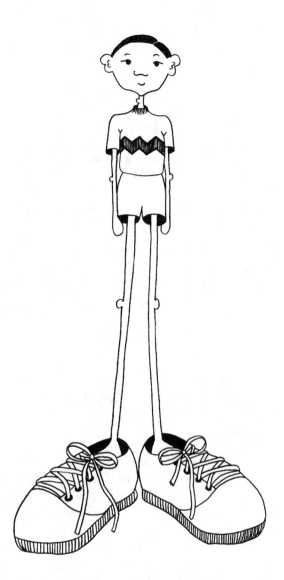

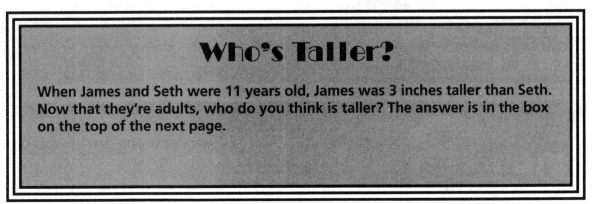

Who's Taller?

When James and Seth were 11 years old, James was 3 inches taller than Seth. Now that they're adults, who do you think is taller? The answer is in the box on the top of the next page.

Keeping Track

Since the height spurt is such an individual thing, why not make your own personal record of growth. Start now by filling in the first line on the chart on this page. Measure yourself every 3 to 6 months and jot down your height on the next line available in the chart.

Taking the Measure of a Man

You won't be able to see changes unless you make accurate measurements. Since it's difficult to measure yourself accurately, we suggest you get one of your parents or someone else to help you.

It's best to measure yourself against a wall or doorframe with your heels, bottom, and shoulder blades pressed against the surface. Stand in the same place each time, so variations in the floor won't mess up your measurement. Measure yourself with your shoes off.

When you're being measured, look straight ahead. Have your helper check to make sure your chin is level and mark your height on the wall or doorframe. Then measure the distance to the floor using the same measuring instrument (tape measure, yardstick) each time.

Your Growth Record

Date	Height	
	feet	inches
	feet	inches
	feet	inches
	feet	inches
	feet	inches
	feet	inches
	feet	inches
	feet	inches
	feet	inches
	feet	inches
	feet	inches
	feet	inches
	feet	inches
	feet	inches
	feet	inches
	feet	inches

How Tall Will I Be?

This is a big question for a lot of boys, and an easy answer is a tall order. We searched high and low for an answer, but there just isn't any easy way to know for certain how tall you'll be when you grow up. There are some clues, though, that can help you make a good "guesstimate" (a cross between a guess and an estimate).

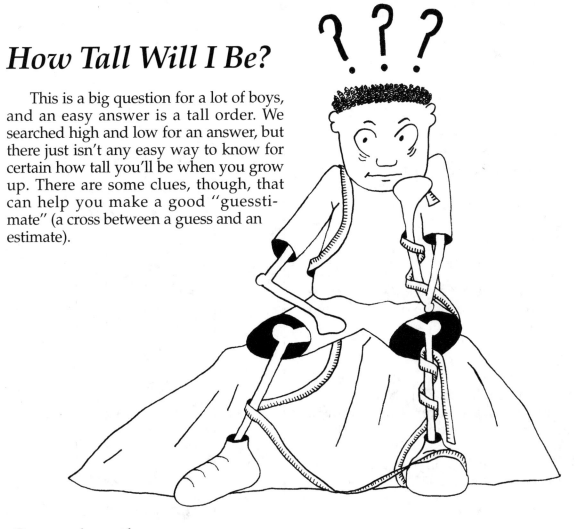

Guesstimating

The three clues on the following pages will help you guesstimate your adult height. For Clue 1, you need to know your height at age 10. For Clue 2 you need your height at age 14. For Clue 3 you need to know your mother's and your father's present heights. (It has to be your birth mother and birth father; step-parents and adoptive parents won't do for this clue.) If you don't have the information needed for all three clues, just do the ones you can. If you're not yet 10, come back and do Clue 1 when you reach your tenth birthday. If you're not yet 14, come back to Clue 2 when you are. Note: If you have enough information to do two or more clues, don't be surprised if you come up with two different answers. (We told you these are only guesstimates.) One hint, though: Clue 1 will give you a more accurate guesstimate of your adult height than Clue 2.

Clue 1

If you know your height on or around your tenth birthday, check out the special ruler on this page. The left-hand (shaded) side of the ruler is marked for a 10-year-old's height. The right-hand side of the ruler shows the corresponding adult heights. To estimate how tall you'll be when you're all grown, just follow these two simple steps:

STEP 1
Find your height at age 10 on the left-hand (shaded) side of the ruler and put a circle around it.

STEP 2
Now, staying on the same line as the height you circled in Step 1, look at the other side of the ruler. Put a square around the height you see there. That's your estimated adult height. For example, if you circled 4'6" in Step 1, then your estimated adult height is 5'9".

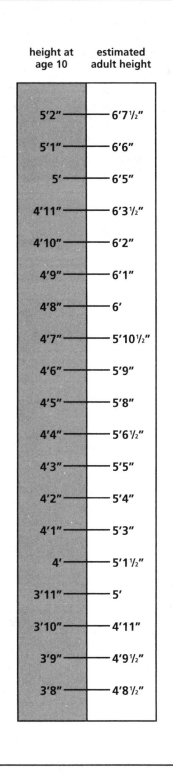

height at age 10	estimated adult height
5'2"	6'7½"
5'1"	6'6"
5'	6'5"
4'11"	6'3½"
4'10"	6'2"
4'9"	6'1"
4'8"	6'
4'7"	5'10½"
4'6"	5'9"
4'5"	5'8"
4'4"	5'6½"
4'3"	5'5"
4'2"	5'4"
4'1"	5'3"
4'	5'1½"
3'11"	5'
3'10"	4'11"
3'9"	4'9½"
3'8"	4'8½"

Clue 2

If you know your height on or around your fourteenth birthday, this is the clue for you. On the special ruler on this page, the left-hand (shaded) side is marked for a 14-year-old's height. The right-hand side of the ruler shows the corresponding adult heights. To estimate how tall you'll be when you're all grown, just follow these two simple steps:

STEP 1

Find your height at age 14 on the left-hand (shaded) side of the ruler and put a circle around it.

STEP 2

Now, staying on the same line as the height you circled in Step 1, look at the other side of the ruler. Put a square around the height you see there. That's your estimated adult height.

For example, if you circled 5'4" in Step 1, your estimated adult height is 5'10".

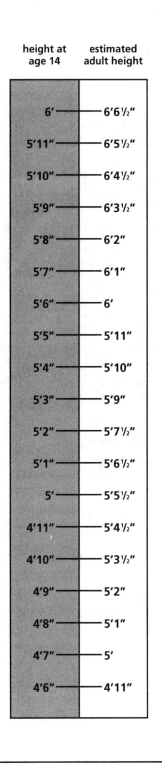

height at age 14	estimated adult height
6'	6'6½"
5'11"	6'5½"
5'10"	6'4½"
5'9"	6'3½"
5'8"	6'2"
5'7"	6'1"
5'6"	6'
5'5"	5'11"
5'4"	5'10"
5'3"	5'9"
5'2"	5'7½"
5'1"	5'6½"
5'	5'5½"
4'11"	5'4½"
4'10"	5'3½"
4'9"	5'2"
4'8"	5'1"
4'7"	5'
4'6"	4'11"

Clue 3

For this clue you'll need to know your mother's and father's present heights in inches. (Remember, birth parents only for this clue.) They'll probably give you their heights in feet and inches. You'll need to convert these measurements to inches. The special ruler on this page will help you do this. The left-hand (shaded) side of the ruler shows feet and inches; the right-hand side shows what these measurements are when converted to inches.

STEP 1

Mark your dad's height in feet and inches on the left-hand (shaded) side of the ruler. To convert his height to inches, just follow the line you marked across to the right-hand side of the ruler. The number you see there is your dad's height in inches. Write that number in the square below and in the square under Step 3 as well.

EXAMPLE: Owen's dad is 6'1" tall. Owen marks this on the ruler and sees that his dad's height in inches is 73 inches.

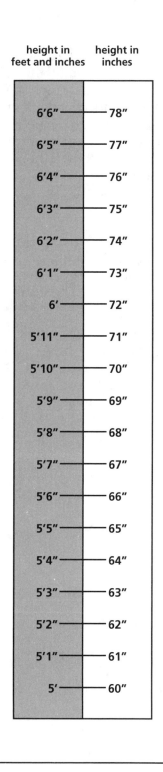

height in feet and inches	height in inches
6'6"	78"
6'5"	77"
6'4"	76"
6'3"	75"
6'2"	74"
6'1"	73"
6'	72"
5'11"	71"
5'10"	70"
5'9"	69"
5'8"	68"
5'7"	67"
5'6"	66"
5'5"	65"
5'4"	64"
5'3"	63"
5'2"	62"
5'1"	61"
5'	60"

STEP 2

Now do the same with your mom. Mark her height in feet and inches on the left-hand (shaded) side of the ruler. Staying on the same line you just marked, look at the right-hand side of the ruler. The number you see there is your mom's height in inches. Write that number in the circle below and in the circle under Step 3 as well.

EXAMPLE: Owen's mom is 5'6" tall. He marks her height on the ruler and sees that she is 66 inches.

STEP 3

Now add the number in the square to the number in the circle and write the answer in the triangle below and in the triangle under Step 4.

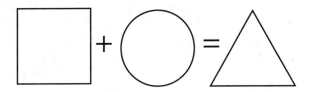

EXAMPLE: Owen adds 73 to 66 and his answer is 139.

STEP 4

Divide the number in the triangle by 2. Write the answer in the diamond below and in the diamond under Step 5.

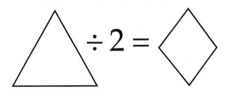

EXAMPLE: When Owen divides 139 by 2, he sees that the answer is $69\frac{1}{2}$.

STEP 5

Now add $2\frac{1}{2}$ inches to the number in the diamond. The result is your estimated adult height in inches.

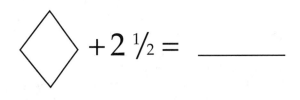

EXAMPLE: Owen adds $69\frac{1}{2}$ inches to $2\frac{1}{2}$ inches for a total of 72 inches. So Owen's estimated adult height is 72 inches.

STEP 6

Now use the ruler to convert your answer from inches to feet and inches. Look at the right-hand side of the ruler to find the number closest to your estimated adult height in inches. Staying on the same line, look at the left-hand (shaded) side of the ruler. The number you see there is your estimated height as an adult in feet and inches. Write your estimated adult height in the star below:

EXAMPLE: Owen looks up 72 inches on the right side of the ruler and sees that this corresponds to 6 feet tall on the left side of the ruler. So, Owen estimates that he will be 6 feet tall once he's finished growing.

Medical Update:
Growing Problems

GROWING PAINS—Muscle pains that come and go, most commonly in legs, thighs, and behind the knees, but sometimes in the arms, back, groin, shoulders, or ankles as well. The pains usually happen in late afternoon and evening. They affect 5- to 13-year-olds and in boys are most common in 13-year-olds.

The cause is unknown, but some experts believe the pains are due to strain produced because the bones are growing faster than the muscles.

If you have this type of pain, check it out with a doctor. Growing pains don't require medical treatment, but you should make sure that you're really having growing pains and not something more serious.

Treatment: Massages, a heating pad, and nonaspirin pain reliever.*

OSGOOD-SCHLATTER DISEASE—A fairly common problem that causes knee pain and swelling. It affects the upper portion of the shin (lower leg) bone, which is still fairly soft, as it doesn't fully harden until you're an adult. Rapid growth during puberty can cause muscles to pull and strain against the soft bone, causing pain and swelling around the knee. This condition is most often seen in boys around the age of 12 to 13. If you develop symptoms, see your doctor.

Treatment: Mild sufferers—lay off vigorous sports and exercises that stress the knee for 2 to 4 weeks; severe cases—the knee needs to rest for several months to a year; very severe cases—a cast may be used to help the knee heal.

SCOLIOSIS—Curving of the spine. It's most likely to occur during the growth spurt, but is more common in girls than in boys.

It's not painful; but if it's not treated, the spine may curve permanently, limiting physical activity. The good news is that it's correctable, especially when caught early.

Symptoms: An S-shaped curve to spine when you bend over, uneven shoulders or hips, shoulder blades that stick out more than normal.

Treatment: Mild cases—special exercises; severe cases—a back brace for a time; very severe cases—usually surgery.

The earlier it's diagnosed, the better. So get checked out by your doctor or school nurse on your next visit.

SLIPPED CAPITAL FEMORAL EPI-PHYSIS—A rare condition in which the growing end of the thigh bone (the femur) has slipped from its normal position. It's more common just before or during rapid growth and happens most often in boys between the ages of 11–13. About 70% of the people who develop this problem are overweight.

Symptoms: Pain in the knee, hip, thigh, and/or groin; a "click" in the hip; a leg that turns outward; or, in some cases, a limp.

If you have symptoms (especially if you have a limp) see a doctor right away. An operation is needed, and the earlier the better.

*Aspirin can cause serious problems for people under 15 years of age.

I.Q.

With This

P.Q.

(puberty quiz)

True	False	
___	___	**1.** As a general rule, boys who are on the short side throughout childhood will also be shorter than average when they reach their adult height.
___	___	**2.** The growth spurt happens at different ages in different boys and is more noticeable in some boys than in others.
___	___	**3.** Girls go through a growth spurt too, but theirs usually starts earlier than boys' and ends earlier.
___	___	**4.** The average 11-year-old girl is taller than the average 11-year-old boy.
___	___	**5.** The growth spurt affects the bones in your upper body and legs before it affects your feet.
___	___	**6.** The legs start the growth spurt before the trunk (the part of your body between your neck and the top of your legs).
___	___	**7.** The growth spurt usually starts around the time you reach Stage 3 of genital development.
___	___	**8.** Most boys are in Stage 4 of development when they reach the peak of their height spurt and are growing at the fastest rate.
___	___	**9.** Growth in height is usually fastest in the spring and summer.

Turn to the next page to see how you did!

ANSWERS

• •

1. **True.** But it's not an unbroken rule. It is true that boys who are short in childhood are usually short as adults, but this is not always the case. Some boys start out shorter than their classmates but find that during puberty, they catch up or even surpass their classmates in height.

2. **True.** Boys may start their growth spurt as young as 10½ years of age or not until they're 16½, and there are some who start even earlier or later than this. A boy may grow a few inches, or he may grow several inches during his growth spurt.

3. **True.** Girls have growth spurts too, but the boys' growth spurt usually starts later and lasts longer than the girls'.

4. **True.** This is because the average girl starts her growth spurt two years before the average boy starts his. But eventually boys catch up and generally wind up being taller than girls.

5. **False.** It's the other way around—feet first.

6. **True.** But the trunk grows more.

7. **True.** The growth spurt usually starts around the same time that the penis begins to grow longer, which is the beginning of Stage 3 of development. This is usually about 1 year after testicle growth (Stage 2).

8. **True.** However, almost one-quarter (25 percent) of boys don't reach their top growth until they're in Stage 5.

9. **True.** This is true for all ages, not just puberty.

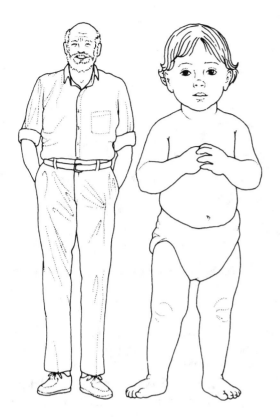

changes the proportions of our bodies (the size of certain parts of the body in comparison with others or with the body as a whole).

During puberty, the legs and the trunk of the body grow much more than the head, and our bodies begin to take on more adult proportions. In boys, there's also more growth in the shoulders than the hips, making the hips seem narrower in comparison and giving your body more "manly" proportions.

For example, in babies, the head accounts for about $\frac{1}{4}$ of the total length of the body and the legs for about $\frac{3}{8}$. But the head doesn't grow nearly as much as the legs do, and by the time we're adults, our proportions have changed quite a bit. In adults, the head is only $\frac{1}{7}$ of the total height, while the legs account for about $\frac{1}{2}$ of our height.

If our proportions didn't change, we'd wind up looking like giant babies!

Are Grown-Ups Big Babies?

If growing up were simply a matter of getting bigger, adults would just be giant babies. Okay, maybe you know some grown-ups who act like big babies, but how many do you know who look like giant babies?

None, of course, because we don't simply enlarge as we grow. Some parts of the body grow more than others. This

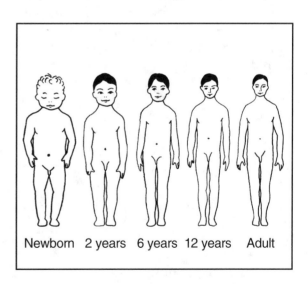

Newborn 2 years 6 years 12 years Adult

To show how proportions change, we have drawn the male body at different ages as if they were equal in height.

These are photos of the same boy taken at different stages of puberty. As you can see, a boy's face changes quite a bit as he grows.

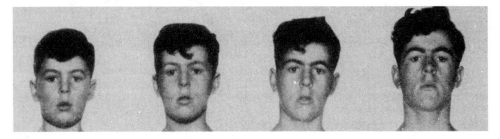

From J. M. Tanner, *Growth at Adolescence* (Oxford: Blackwell Scientific Publications, 1962). Used with permission.

Your Changing Face

The puberty growth spurt also affects the bones in your head and face. The head increases somewhat in size, but the more dramatic changes occur in the face. The face becomes longer, and its proportions change. The overall effect is that your face is narrower and less pudgy than it was when you were a kid.

Some bones grow more than others. Although the entire face lengthens, the greatest increase is in the lower portion. One result is that your chin juts out more.

Your nose gets longer and wider and becomes more prominent. It reaches its adult size before the rest of your facial features. So if you feel as if your nose is too big for your face, it may be that the rest of your features just need a little time to catch up.

Your mouth also widens, and your lips become fuller. Your forehead is higher and wider, and the entire profile is straighter.

In some boys, these changes are quite dramatic; in others, they are less noticeable. Because you see yourself in the mirror each day, even dramatic changes may not be very obvious to you. The exercises on the next couple of pages will make you more aware of how facial features change during puberty.

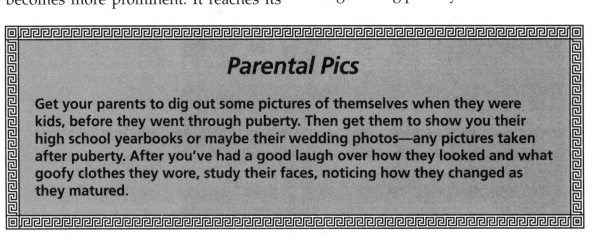

Parental Pics

Get your parents to dig out some pictures of themselves when they were kids, before they went through puberty. Then get them to show you their high school yearbooks or maybe their wedding photos—any pictures taken after puberty. After you've had a good laugh over how they looked and what goofy clothes they wore, study their faces, noticing how they changed as they matured.

Face Matchups

Just to give you an idea of how much faces can change during puberty, we gathered together some "before-and-after-puberty" pictures. See if you can guess which kid turned into which adult by drawing a line connecting the pictures that go together.

The correct answers are printed upside down at the bottom of the page.

1.

2.

3.

a.

b.

c.

Answers: Number 1 grew up to be b; number 2 grew up to be c; number 3 grew up to be a.

Picture Yourself Changing

Paste in photos of yourself taken every six months or so. It'll be easier to see how much you've changed if you use the same camera and stand about the same distance from the camera for each picture. Photos from a coin-operated booth are great for showing the changes in your face. Or you might use photos that show your whole body.

Each time you add another photo to the page, write the date the picture was taken underneath it.

Weight Spurt

Not only do you grow taller faster during the puberty growth spurt, you also put on pounds at a faster rate. In fact, at the peak of the weight spurt (typically about age 14 or 15), it's not unusual for a boy to gain as many as 25 pounds in a single year. The weight spurt lasts for 2 to 3 years, and the average boy adds about 45 pounds during this time.

Part of this weight gain is due to the longer, thicker bones that you develop at puberty. But a large part of the weight gain is the result of muscle development.

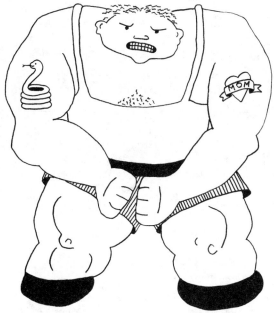

Muscle Development & Strength

A boy's muscles also go through a growth spurt during puberty. Both the size and the number of muscle cells increase, so that the amount of muscle in a boy's body doubles during his muscle spurt.

Along with this muscle growth comes an increase in strength, but not right away. The muscle, weight, and height spurts all happen at about the same time. But the increase in strength trails behind by about a year.

Once strength does begin to increase, a boy's ability to lift, throw, hit, run, and jump improves. Because muscles in the shoulders, back, and chest are larger, the strength of arm pull and push (thrust) is increased. So is the strength of the hand grip. A boy's reaction time and muscle coordination improve as well.

This isn't simply a matter of having more muscles. The lungs and heart also grow larger and work more efficiently, which means greater endurance and quicker recovery from the effects of exercise.

Superman You Won't Be

If we're giving you the idea that puberty turns boys into hunks with masses of bulging muscles or enables them to leap tall buildings, we don't mean to. Each of us is different, and how our bodies develop is influenced by many things: what we eat, how much sleep and exercise we get, our general health, and our family background (what we've inherited from our parents and grandparents). How we develop is also a matter of basic body types. Turn the page to learn about yours.

What's Your Basic Body Type?

The three basic body types are shown here. Each of us has at least some characteristics of each type. Some people are almost purely one of the three and have hardly any characteristics of the other two types. Depending on their bodies, such people are said to be classic endomorphs, classic ectomorphs, or classic mesomorphs.

Other people have a more even balance of traits from each body type. But no one has a perfectly even balance, and every adult can be classified into one of the three basic types.

It's harder to classify young people because their bodies are changing so much, but see if you can identify your body type. Read the descriptions of each type, and put a check mark next to the body type that is closest to yours.

❑ **Endomorphs** tend to be round and stocky, with round heads, short, thick necks, more body fat, and short arms and legs. Classic endomorphs may start puberty early, but finish late.

❑ **Ectomorphs** tend to be thin and angular, with narrow bodies, little body fat, thin arms and legs, and long, stringy muscles. Classic ectomorphs tend to go through puberty late.

❑ **Mesomorphs** tend to be strongly built, with broad, muscular chest and shoulders, muscular arms and legs, and little body fat. Classic mesomorphs tend to go through puberty early.

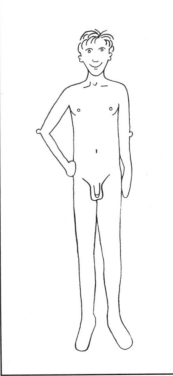

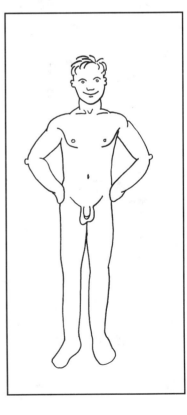

Your Bod

Many of the boys we talked to were not happy with the way their bodies looked and wanted to be thinner, heavier, or more muscular (or totally buff). Some said they wanted to change their bodies by dieting and bodybuilding.

It's true that dieting and exercise can change the shape of the body to some extent, but we each have a basic body type that doesn't change, no matter how much dieting and exercise we do. If you're the endomorphic type, it's important for you to know that you may be at a weight that is the perfectly healthy, ideal weight for you yet look heavier than your friends or classmates who are the same weight but are ectomorphs. By the same token, if you're an ectomorph, you may be slimmer than some of your friends, which is perfectly normal for you.

You should also know that dieting is not necessarily good at your age and that bodybuilding definitely isn't the right type of exercise for people your age.

Exercising Right

There are basically three types of exercise: strength building (bodybuilding), stretching, and aerobic (endurance).

Bodybuilding

If your goal is to be totally buff and muscle-bound, you'll have to wait until you're mostly grown. Before puberty, it's pretty much impossible for a boy to develop big muscles because muscle growth is affected by hormones (the special body chemicals we discussed in Part 3). Before puberty, there just aren't enough of these hormones for you to develop big muscles. Lifting heavy weights before puberty isn't likely to produce the results you're looking for; and in fact, it can hurt you because even if your muscles are strong enough to lift a heavy weight, your bones may not be. You won't snap in half, but you can do long-term damage to your bones.

The ends of your bones are still kind of soft while you're growing. They don't become completely hard until you've reached your full adult height. While these bone ends are soft, repeatedly lifting heavy weights can damage them and cause problems with your natural growth.

Stretching

Stretching exercises help keep your body loose. When you stretch out a muscle, do so gently. Don't bounce up and down; instead, let gravity gently pull and stretch your muscles. Don't overdo it. If you want to stretch a certain part of your body, it's better to stretch a little each day than a lot all at once. Otherwise, you may pull a muscle.

Stretching exercises are mainly important before and after aerobic exercise. Stretching can warm up the muscles before aerobic exercise to make them looser, which decreases the chances of injury. Stretching afterward helps prevent stiffness.

Aerobics

This is the most important kind of exercise. Not only is it good for your muscles; it exercises your heart and lungs, too. Doing these kinds of exercises builds your endurance and helps keep you feeling good and fit.

Examples of aerobic exercises include anything that really gets your heart rate going, like running or walking fast. So, if you're active in track or in team sports, you may be getting this kind of exercise already. But sitting on the bench doesn't count. You have to be actively exercising in order to get the benefits of aerobic exercise. Experts say you should do some sort of aerobic exercise for at least 20 minutes, three times a week.

Even if you're not into sports, even if you're a total klutz, you can still get the exercise you need. Take a brisk walk or ride a bike (but you have to actually peddle for the 20 minutes; no coasting). There are lots of things you can do to keep that heart rate up for the full 20 minutes.

Dieting

Dieting is a bad idea for people your age. Your body needs lots of energy to grow, and you don't want to risk denying it the nutrients and vitamins it needs. But even if you can't diet, you can eat smart! You should exercise regularly and make sure you're eating the right amounts of the right foods so your body has what it needs to grow.

STEROIDS

Steroids are synthetic forms of the male hormone testosterone. Some people take these drugs because they can make the body build up muscles faster than is normal. But steroids are very dangerous, especially for teens, because they can interfere with your body's normal development. Besides, steroids work only while you're taking them. As soon as you stop, the muscles disappear. Steroids just aren't a good idea. If you really want to build muscles, you can get long-lasting and positive effects with proper exercise.

Some side effects of using steroids show up after only a few months:

Normal growth stops
Bad acne
Overly aggressive behavior
Testicles shrink
Breasts enlarge
Headaches, dizziness,
    nosebleeds

Others may show up months or years later:

Heart attack
Cancer
Baldness
Personality changes
Mental problems

Eating Right

A healthy diet is important, especially while you're growing. To stay healthy, you should eat reasonable amounts of a variety of foods. And no, we don't mean snack foods. You need to eat foods from all four basic food groups each day. We've listed the four basic food groups and how much you should eat from each group every day.

Meat and Other Protein-Rich Foods
- Three 2-ounce servings daily.

This category includes all meat (beef, lamb, pork, poultry) as well as other foods that are high in protein (like fish, seafood, eggs, beans, and peanut butter).

Fruits and Vegetables
- Four or more servings daily; one serving = 1 piece of fresh fruit or ½ cup cooked fruit or vegetables.

This category is especially important because it provides you with a lot of vitamins without a lot of fat or calories. Also, fruit can make a really good substitute for sugary snacks. You should note, though, that not all vegetables count as vegetables. Some of them (like potatoes) count as starches instead.

Breads, Pasta, Cereal, and Starchy Vegetables
- Four or more servings daily; one serving = 1 slice of bread or ½ cup cooked pasta, starchy vegetables, or cereal.

Notice that some vegetables count as starches instead of as vegetables. Examples of these include potatoes, corn, carrots, peas, and onions.

The foods in this category contain carbohydrates, which give you energy. Everyone needs to eat these starchy foods to maintain their energy levels. But if you're trying to watch your weight, don't eat a lot more of these than the daily requirement. These foods can add weight if eaten a lot. This is especially true because we often eat them with spreads or sauces that contain a lot of fat (like putting lots of butter on your potato or a cream sauce on your pasta). On the other hand, if adding weight is your goal, this is the stuff for you!

Milk and Milk Products
- Two to three 1-cup servings daily.

This category doesn't just include milk; it also includes stuff made from milk, like yogurt, cheese, and—you guessed it—ice cream! But that doesn't mean you can eat 3 cups of ice cream a day and consider yourself healthy. Being healthy means not only eating the daily requirement from each food group, but also eating a variety of foods within each category. To make sure you're getting a good mix, fill in the chart on the next page.

My Daily Intake

Use the charts below to keep track of what you eat for one week. Each time you eat a serving from one of the food groups, put a check in one of the boxes for that day.

Monday
Meat & Proteins	Fruits & Vegetables	Breads, Etc.	Milk & Its Products
☐ ☐ ☐	☐ ☐ ☐ ☐	☐ ☐ ☐ ☐	☐ ☐ ☐

Tuesday
Meat & Proteins	Fruits & Vegetables	Breads, Etc.	Milk & Its Products
☐ ☐ ☐	☐ ☐ ☐ ☐	☐ ☐ ☐ ☐	☐ ☐ ☐

Wednesday
Meat & Proteins	Fruits & Vegetables	Breads, Etc.	Milk & Its Products
☐ ☐ ☐	☐ ☐ ☐ ☐	☐ ☐ ☐ ☐	☐ ☐ ☐

Thursday
Meat & Proteins	Fruits & Vegetables	Breads, Etc.	Milk & Its Products
☐ ☐ ☐	☐ ☐ ☐ ☐	☐ ☐ ☐ ☐	☐ ☐ ☐

Friday
Meat & Proteins	Fruits & Vegetables	Breads, Etc.	Milk & Its Products
☐ ☐ ☐	☐ ☐ ☐ ☐	☐ ☐ ☐ ☐	☐ ☐ ☐

Saturday
Meat & Proteins	Fruits & Vegetables	Breads, Etc.	Milk & Its Products
☐ ☐ ☐	☐ ☐ ☐ ☐	☐ ☐ ☐ ☐	☐ ☐ ☐

Sunday
Meat & Proteins	Fruits & Vegetables	Breads, Etc.	Milk & Its Products
☐ ☐ ☐	☐ ☐ ☐ ☐	☐ ☐ ☐ ☐	☐ ☐ ☐

B.O. & Zits
Is Puberty
The Pits?

PART FIVE

No, puberty won't turn you into a smelly, pimply greaseball, though books, pamphlets, and videos for boys your age make it sound that way. You know the kind we mean—the ones that go on and on about "personal hygiene." They can make you feel really paranoid about B.O. (body odor), like you'll need to soak in a vat of deodorant every day. Or they make it seem that if you don't wash your face ten times a day and coat yourself with pimple cream, you'll be a permanent resident of Zit City.

On the one hand, puberty brings new body hair and the first facial hair, and some boys are excited about this. But it's also true that during puberty your perspiration (sweat) glands become more active, so you perspire more and develop an adult body odor. Oil glands in the skin of the scalp, face, feet, and elsewhere become more active too, and you may notice that the hair on your head is more oily or that you have more pimples.

Let's face it, you could probably live without these and some of the other changes in this chapter, but it's part of the package. Before you panic, read the information and try the activities and exercises in this section. They'll teach you the facts about these changes and how to cope with them.

Perspiration & Body Odor (Sweat & B.O.)

During puberty, your perspiration glands become more active, and your body chemistry changes so that you develop a more adult body odor. You perspire in the areas of your body that have more of these glands—under your arms, the palms of your hands, the bottoms of your feet, and the genitals. Perspiration is healthy, so let it pore! Washing your body daily and wearing clean clothes will help prevent body odor. Deodorant soaps can be particularly helpful. If odor or wetness is a problem, you can use an underarm deodorant to control odor or an antiperspirant to help control perspiration and cut down on wetness. These are available separately or combined in the same product. Baking soda can also be used under the arms to absorb wetness and odor. It's important to remember, though, that deodorants and powders are not substitutes for soap and water!

Foot Odor

If we all ran around barefoot, foot odor wouldn't be a problem. The gallon or so of perspiration our feet produce each week would simply evaporate into the air. But we wear shoes, which trap all that sweat close to our feet. This provides a warm, moist place for bacteria to grow. It's the bacteria that cause that rotten egg, sulfur scent on your feet and shoes. So what do you do? Here are some suggestions for taming the problem.

■ *Don't wear the same shoes every day.* Shoes should have at least 24 hours to air out between wearings.

■ *Wear absorbent socks.* Natural fibers, like cotton, absorb moisture and allow air to circulate.

■ *Avoid shoes with synthetic fibers.* Stick to natural fibers like canvas or leather because they let more air in and out of the shoe. This keeps your feet cooler and dryer and makes them a less attractive home for bacteria.

■ *Powders or sprays for the feet or shoes and special deodorizing shoe inserts may help.* These products are available in most drugstores or pharmacies, but your best bet is to avoid letting the bacteria build up in the first place.

■ *Toss washable shoes in the laundry.* This can help, but it may not solve your problem.

■ *Keep your feet clean and dry.* Make sure that you dry them well, especially between the toes! Keeping the feet and shoes clean and dry is your best bet for fighting those smelly bacteria!

Pimples & Acne

Zits, whiteheads, blackheads—if they don't sound like a lot of fun, that's because they aren't. Unfortunately, they're very common during puberty; eight out of every ten teens develop pimples or acne.

During puberty, oil glands beneath the surface of the skin grow larger and begin making more *sebum,* a white, oily substance that keeps the skin moist. The sebum can get backed up in the ducts of the enlarged oil glands and cause whiteheads or blackheads. Pimples can become infected, resulting in red, swollen, pus-filled ducts. The infection may break through the walls of the ducts, causing a more severe acne problem.

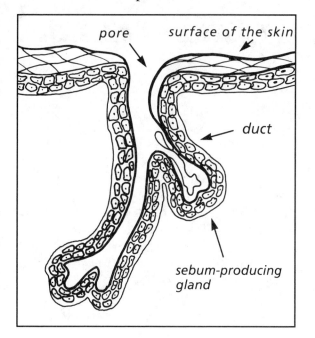

pore

surface of the skin

duct

sebum-producing gland

Many people have the mistaken idea that blackheads and acne are caused by tiny dirt particles beneath the skin and that washing your face several times a day will prevent these skin problems. Not true!

When sebum comes into contact with air, it may turn black; and it's this, not dirt, that causes the dark color of blackheads. Washing your face twice a day will help remove dirt and dead cells that would add to acne problems. But washing only affects the surface of your skin; acne is caused by what happens *under* the surface of your skin. You could wash your face a hundred times a day, but it wouldn't keep you from getting acne. In fact, washing too often may make the problem worse by irritating the skin and drying it out. This, in turn, causes the oil glands to produce even more sebum, which can lead to even more acne! And we hate to give you the bad news, guys, but males are much more likely to have acne problems than females.

So what's a guy to do? Fear not, there is help as close as your local drugstore. Check out the next page for information on how to deal with those little buggers if they show up on you. If you have a particularly severe case of acne and over-the-counter medications don't clear it up, don't just sit back and take it. Go see a skin doctor (called a *dermatologist*), who can help you. Don't suffer in silence; acne is a very treatable problem.

Acne Do's and Don'ts

- DON'T use oily sunscreens or lotions on problem areas. If you want to know if a skin product is okay to use, look for the word *noncomedogenic* on the label.

- DO wash your face regularly to avoid adding to an acne problem, but don't overwash or dry out the skin. Washing twice a day should suffice.

- DON'T squeeze any form of acne as this can make the problem worse and can even cause scars!

- DO keep a good mental attitude. Pimples are a drag, but they are perfectly normal. Try to keep a positive outlook and don't let those little buggers stop you from doing the things you want to do.

Acne Medications

There are a variety of acne treatments you can buy over-the-counter, without a doctor's prescription. Look for products that contain one of the following two acne-fighting ingredients.

BENZOYL PEROXIDE

The most common over-the-counter medication, it helps to fight acne by opening pores and killing the bacteria that cause the inflammation in a pimple. It makes skin feel tight and dry, but too much can be irritating to skin, so follow directions and don't overdo it.

SALICYLIC ACID

This medication is less irritating than benzoyl peroxide and even better at dealing with blackheads. So if blackheads are your problem, this may be the stuff for you. Salicylic acid doesn't kill bacteria the way benzoyl peroxide does, but it is an anti-inflammatory, which means it cuts down on the inflammation associated with pimples.

If the over-the-counter products don't work, there are a number of effective medical treatments. See your doctor or a a dermatologist for more information.

Test Your

I.Q.

With This

P.Q.
(puberty quiz)

True   **False**

1. If you have pimples during puberty, you'll probably have them all your life.

2. Being nervous or excited can cause our perspiration and oil glands to become more active, which in turn may cause more perspiration and pimples.

3. Boys are more apt to have pimples during puberty than girls.

4. Blackheads are caused by little pieces of dirt under the skin.

5. A good way of getting rid of pimples is to squeeze or pop them.

6. Clean skin doesn't break out.

7. There is no medical treatment for acne.

8. Eating chocolate or greasy foods causes pimples and acne.

9. Acne is hereditary, meaning that it runs in families.

Turn to the next page to see how you did!

ANSWERS

· ·

1. **False.** Although some people have skin problems all their lives, most of us tend to outgrow our pimples by the time we reach our late teens or early twenties.

2. **True.** Nervousness, excitement, or stress can cause an increase in perspiration and pimples.

3. **True.** Boys usually have more trouble with pimple during puberty than girls do.

4. **False.** Blackheads happen because the oils that clog the skin's pores turn black when they come in contact with the oxygen in the air around us. Blackheads are not caused by dirt particles under the skin.

5. **False.** Squeezing a pimple pushes infected pus into the surrounding skin and can cause severe break-outs of acne and may result in permanent scarring. (African-American boys be sure to read page 88.)

6. **False.** Acne is the result of things happening under the skin's surface, so even clean skin can have acne.

7. **False.** Although acne isn't 100 percent curable, it can be treated successfully with over-the-counter medications or with the help of a skilled dermatologist (skin doctor).

8. **False.** Most doctors agree that eating chocolate or greasy foods does not increase your chances of getting acne. However, some people may be especially sensitive to certain foods, so if you notice that you tend to have more breakouts in the week following eating a certain type of food, try eliminating it from your diet and see what happens.

9. **True.** Acne does seem to run in families, so if your parents or older brothers and sisters had acne, you may be more likely to develop it.

Underarm & Other Body Hair

The word *puberty* comes from the Latin word *pubescere*, which means "to be covered with hair." Actually, most of the body is covered by fine, short, colorless villous hairs throughout childhood. During puberty, villous hairs are rapidly replaced by adult-type terminal hair, which may have some color to it. How much terminal hair you have, where it grows, and its color are determined by your racial, ethnic, and personal family background.

The curly pubic hair we talked about in Part 2 is a special type of terminal hair that grows on and around the sex organs. During puberty, villous hair in the armpits is also replaced by terminal hair. In addition, you may notice that the hair elsewhere on your body is darker in color, and that there's more of it.

UNDERARM HAIR

Underarm hair usually doesn't begin to grow until a year or two after pubic hair growth begins. But this is not a hard-and-fast rule. For instance, some boys develop underarm hair before they have any pubic hair at all.

At first, underarm hairs are fine, straight, and only slightly colored. It takes about a year before more deeply colored, adult-type hairs appear.

HAIR ON THE ARMS & LEGS

Early in puberty, slightly colored terminal hairs rapidly begin to replace the villous hairs on the arms. Terminal hair growth on the legs usually doesn't start until terminal hair growth on the arms is well under way. As we've said, the amount of hair and its color depend on your family background. Some boys have quite a bit; others have very little.

OTHER BODY HAIR

The hair growth on the upper legs may include the buttocks as well. In addition, some males grow hair on their chests, shoulders, and/or back. Others don't. Either way is perfectly normal.

Facial Hair

The first facial hairs usually appear between the ages of 14 and 16. However, some boys develop facial hair at a younger age, while others don't do so until they're 19 or 20 years old. The hairs usually appear during Stage 4 of development.

The first facial hairs are usually found on the outer corners of the upper lip. At first, they may be only slightly dark in color, and there won't be very many of them. But with time, the color will become deeper, and the mustache will gradually fill in, growing toward the middle of the upper lip. While the mustache is filling in, hair usually grows on the upper portion of the cheeks.

As you mature, your facial hair will get fuller and more deeply colored. Men who hardly had any hair at the age of 20 may have a full beard by age 30. Also, the facial hair may or may not be the same color as the hair on your head. It's a very individual thing.

Some men decide to grow beards and mustaches; others choose to shave their facial hair. Many boys feel very grown-up when they start shaving. You may or may not decide to shave; the choice is yours. If you think you might want to shave, take a look at "A Guy's Guide to Shaving," on the next few pages.

A Guy's Guide to Shaving

Equipment

The first thing you need to decide is what type of razor you're going to use. Basically, you have two choices: a regular blade razor or an electric razor.

BLADE VERSUS ELECTRIC

A blade razor gives a somewhat closer shave, but the big difference is in the "smoothness" of the shave. The blade razor cuts the hair at an angle, leaving only a slight tip of hair. The electric razor cuts nearly as close to the skin, but it lops off the hair straight across, the way a tree trunk is cut, and the cut feels rougher to the touch.

Also, blade razors give a clean shave. The blades scrape dead cells from the skin's surface, so that skin feels especially clean after blade-razor shaving. On the other hand, electric razors are more convenient and less likely to cause nicks and cuts. They also take less oil out of the skin and are a good choice if you have problems with dry or sensitive skin.

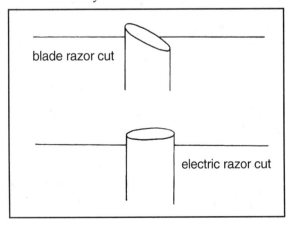

blade razor cut

electric razor cut

ELECTRIC RAZORS

There are two types of electric razor: rotaries and foils. They cost anywhere from about $30 to $100 or more, depending on the design and extra features (cordless, rechargeable, and so forth).

■ *Rotary electric razors* have a series of tiny blades that fan out from a wheel and work on the same principle as a lawn mower. As you move the razor across your face, the whirling blades cut the whiskers.

■ *Foil-type electric razors* have a thin piece of metal (the foil) that has hundreds of tiny holes in it. As you move the razor back and forth on your face, the whiskers poke through the holes and are sheared off by the cutting block that lies beneath the foil.

BLADE RAZORS

There are a number of choices here:

■ *Disposable versus reusable:* The big issue here is the environment. Disposable, or throwaway, razors just add to the mountains of trash we're leaving behind for future generations to deal with.

■ *Single versus double blades:* The double- (twin- or dual-) blade razor has two cutting edges. Single-blade razors have only one cutting edge.

The double blades give a closer shave, but they also scrape off more surface skin and are more likely to cause irritation (especially for those with sensitive skin). You're also more likely to get nicks and cuts using a double blade.

■ *Pivot and flexible heads:* The latest thing in blade razors is a double-blade razor with a cartridge that swivels and blades that ride on tiny springs to give you a closer, more comfortable shave.

Men give these razors top marks according to an article in *Consumer Reports* magazine. But as the article also points out, shaving with one of these razors costs about $25 per year, while other razors rated nearly as high cost only about $16 per year to use.

Shaving, How To

How you shave depends on which type of razor you're using. But whatever razor you use, keep the following things in mind.

■ *Take your time.* If you hurry, you are more likely to nick or cut yourself.

■ *Rinse with cool water.* This will cut down on irritation to the skin.

■ *Don't share your razor or borrow someone else's.* Disease can be passed by sharing razors, so keep it to yourself!

SHAVING WITH A BLADE RAZOR

A man removes 15,000 to 30,000 whiskers when he shaves, and no matter how fine a razor he uses, this daily scraping can be rough on his skin. The following tips will help you avoid many of the skin problems caused by shaving.

■ *Wetter is better.* The secret to a smooth, comfortable shave is softening the whiskers so they're easier to cut. The wiry hair shafts soften when they absorb water. By thoroughly wetting your whiskers before shaving, you can reduce the amount of force needed to cut the whiskers by as much as 70 percent. That's important because too much pressure and razor drag on the skin can cause *razor burn*, a red, stinging rash on the face.

Some experts suggest shaving in the shower (using one of those fog-proof mirrors). Others recommend shaving just after you've showered. Still others advise wetting the face and applying shaving cream or gel and then letting it sit for 5 minutes before you begin to shave.

■ *Use warm (not hot) water.* Warm water works best while you're shaving, but you don't want it too hot. Hot water plumps up the skin, so it's harder to get a close shave and easier to nick yourself. Don't forget to rinse with cool water.

■ *Use a shaving cream, gel, or foam, not soap.* These shaving products help keep the hair and skin soft and reduce the drag of the razor across the skin. This reduces the chances of razor burn and infection. Don't use soap as a lubricant; it clogs the razor and dulls the blade. Besides, soap can dry and irritate the skin.

■   *Use a sharp blade.* Dull blades drag across the skin more roughly and can cause irritation. Also, dull blades don't cut well, so you're tempted to press harder than you would with a sharp blade. Pressing hard increases the irritation to the skin. To make sure you're using sharp blades, you should change them after nine to eleven uses.

■   *Shave in the direction of hair growth.* Shaving against the hair growth may give a closer shave, but it is much more irritating to the skin. For this reason, it's best to shave downward, in the direction of hair growth.

■   *Save the chin and upper lip for last.* Your whiskers are thickest here; so by saving these areas until last, you've given these whiskers that much more time to soften.

■   *Rinse your razor after use, but don't wipe the blade.* Allow your razor to air-dry. Drying the razor with a towel or otherwise wiping the blade dulls it, shortening its life.

SHAVING WITH AN ELECTRIC RAZOR

■   *Shave when your face is dry.* Electrics work best on stiff whiskers, so shave before you shower. You might want to use one of the shaving solutions made for use with electric razors, especially if you have a tough beard. These solutions are

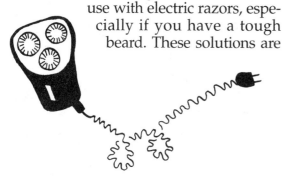

splashed on the face prior to shaving and are allowed to dry (which takes only about 15 seconds) before you begin to shave. They make the whiskers stiffer, which makes for a closer shave.

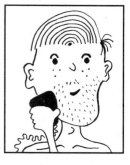

■   *Don't press too hard.* Electric razors are supposed to glide across the face. Pressing harder won't give you a closer shave and could damage the razor heads.

■   *Clean the razor regularly.* Some electrics come with a special brush or tool for cleaning; others simply have to be emptied out or rinsed under the tap. Follow the instructions that come with the razor.

■   *Replace the blades each year.* Most manufacturers of foil and rotary electric razors recommend that the blades be replaced once a year. But here again, follow the instructions that come with your razor.

Nicks, Cuts, & Other Irritations

Everybody who shaves suffers minor cuts or nicks in the skin sooner or later. Since this is more likely to happen when you're new to the art of shaving, it's a good idea to have a *styptic pencil* handy to stop the bleeding.

A styptic pencil isn't really a pencil at

all. It's a wooden stick coated with chemicals that help stop bleeding. You press it against the nick or cut and hold it there while the chemicals do their job. Styptic pencils are sold in drugstores.

If you don't have a styptic pencil handy, apply constant pressure with a clean tissue until the bleeding stops (usually within 3 to 5 minutes). Don't shave the area again until the cut has healed. If redness persists for more than a few days, see your doctor. If you find that you're cutting yourself all the time, switch to an electric razor.

RAZOR BURN

Razor burn is a red, itchy, irritated, inflamed condition that sometimes results from shaving with too dull a blade or pressing too hard while shaving. If you get it, you'll know because it hurts. Usually it goes away by itself, but if it doesn't go away after a few days, see your doctor because it can become infected. Let the area heal before you shave there again.

IN-GROWN HAIRS

These can happen to anyone, but they are especially common in African-Americans and people with really curly hair. If you're African-American or have super-curly hair, read the in-grown hair section on page 88.

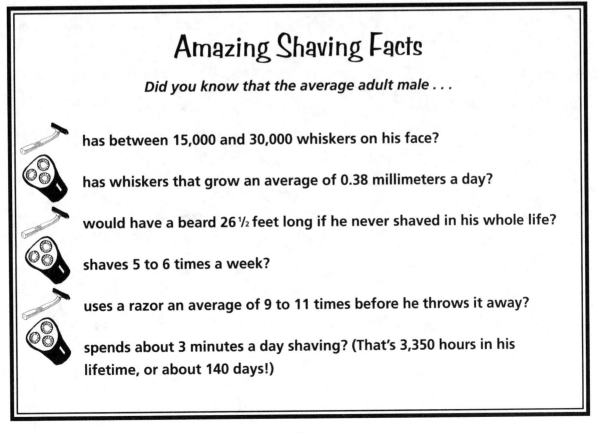

Amazing Shaving Facts

Did you know that the average adult male . . .

has between 15,000 and 30,000 whiskers on his face?

has whiskers that grow an average of 0.38 millimeters a day?

would have a beard 26 ½ feet long if he never shaved in his whole life?

shaves 5 to 6 times a week?

uses a razor an average of 9 to 11 times before he throws it away?

spends about 3 minutes a day shaving? (That's 3,350 hours in his lifetime, or about 140 days!)

Ask a Man Who Knows

Your dad or another adult man you trust will have some helpful advice about shaving. Ask a man who knows the following questions:

1. How old were you when you started shaving?_____

2. What did you use to shave with the first time? Did someone show you how, or did you just pick it up on your own?

_____

_____

_____

3. What type of razor and shaving products do you use now and why?

_____

_____

_____

4. Have you used other types of razors or shaving products in the past? If so what did you use, how did you like them, and why did you stop using them?

_____

_____

5. What advice do you have for me?

_____

_____

Racewriting

You've gotten a lot of information about shaving! Do you have any thoughts about whether or not you'd like to shave? Why or why not? What helped you make your decision? If you decide that you do want to shave, what kind of razor do you think you'd like to try? Are you looking forward to the day when you grow facial hair, or do you think it sounds like a drag? If you've already grown some facial hair, how did you feel when you first noticed it? What questions do you still have? What are you feeling right now?

Remember to write as fast as you can, and don't stop for anything! Get your watch ready so you can fill in your time at the end. Ready, set, GO!

write your time here

Special Concerns for African-American Men

Shaving and treatments for pimples and acne can pose special problems for African-Americans. Here's how and why and what you can do to avoid these problems.

ABRASIVE SOAPS AND SCRUBS

Don't use them! They won't clear up your acne, and they may discolor dark complexions, causing patches of permanently lightened or darkened skin.

IN-GROWN HAIRS

Because their hair is so strong and curly, African-Americans—especially those who shave —are more likely to have problems with in-grown hairs which cause irritation and bumps on the skin. Sometimes the hair will free itself, but it's best to free the tip of the hair from the skin if you can. DO NOT pluck the hair out entirely, though. This may cause even worse problems under the skin.

Shaving can make matters worse. Shaving puts tension on the skin and cuts the hair at an angle, leaving a sharp tip. Once the tension is relaxed, the hair can retract beneath the skin's surface, causing inflamed, irritated bumps on the surface of the skin. In some cases, these become infected and form large cysts, or collections of fluid, under the skin.

Shaving against the grain, with a double blade razor, or with a dull razor can make the problem worse. Electric razors don't help much because they're designed for straight hair.

The best way to avoid the problem is not to shave at all. If you don't want a

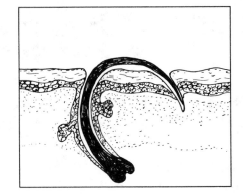

In-Grown Hairs: The tip of a curly hair can loop back, pierce the skin's surface and grow inward. Shaving cuts hair to sharp tips and increases the likelihood of developing in-grown hairs.

beard or mustache, another solution is to cut the hair close to the skin with hair clippers, leaving a little stubble and a five-o'clock-shadow look. Some African-American men occasionally use chemical hair removers; but in order to remove the hair, African-Americans may have to leave the chemicals on the skin for a long time, which means they have more chance to irritate the skin. If you use a chemical hair remover, *always* test a small patch of skin before using the cream. Use cream removers with moisturizers and natural herbs and oils (aloe, yarrow, rosemary, sage). Stay out of the sun, chlorine, and salt water for 24 hours after applying these products.

KELOID PROBLEMS

African-American skin is more likely to form abnormal scars known as *keloids*. Scar tissue is formed as a part of the healing process when there's a cut, wound, or other damage to the skin. But in people subject to keloid problems, scar tissue continues to form even after the injury has healed, resulting in an extra build-up of tissue. The person is left with a raised, oddly shaped scar that may itch a lot. Even a little nick from shaving or popping a pimple can leave a noticeable scar in a person subject to keloids. Because of the risk of razor cuts and scarring from in-grown hairs, boys with keloids should consult their doctors before attempting to shave.

Voice Changes

During puberty, the larynx (voice box) grows larger and a boy's vocal cords become thicker and longer, changing the tone of his voice. A boy's voice deepens and begins to sound like a grown man's.

Girls' voices change too, though not as much as boys' voices. Male hormones cause boys' voice boxes and vocal cords to grow more than girls' do. In fact, males' vocal cords wind up being three times as long as females'.

Voice changes usually happen when a boy is about 14 or 15 years old, but it's perfectly normal for these changes to happen earlier or later than this. Your voice may change rather abruptly or it may happen without your really noticing it.

While their voices are changing, some boys experience voice "cracking." When a boy's voice "cracks" it suddenly shifts to a higher pitch, and temporarily sounds high and squeaky. Some of the boys and men we talked to say this was the most embarrassing thing that happened to them during adolescence. Others said it was no big deal. If your voice does crack, try not to worry about it. It's just another sign that you're growing up. You may also want to take a look at the quotes on this page to see what some other boys and men had to say about voice changes.

"I think I was around 15. It was a real brief period where I'd get occasional cracks. You know, it didn't last more than maybe like a month and then from then on my voice just gradually got deeper, but it was a real gradual thing."
—Chris, age 25

"If it cracked, it was no big deal. We all knew what it was, and it was happening to everybody."

Breast Changes

Over half of all males have some breast swelling during puberty, which may be accompanied by soreness and discomfort. The swelling may be more noticeable in some boys than in others. These breast changes are perfectly normal and rarely last more than a year to a year and a half.

There may be a flat, button-like bump under one or both nipples which may be sore or tender. Again, this is temporary. It's part of your body's adjusting to its new hormones and it's perfectly normal.

One change that is permanent is that the areola (the colored patch of skin around the nipple) gets wider and darker during puberty. This may or may not be very noticeable, but again, it's perfectly normal.

Some boys we talked to who have experienced these changes were a little worried. They thought that they might have cancer or something; one boy even said he was afraid he might be turning into a girl! He wasn't, of course. All of these changes are just a natural part of growing up.

Stretch Marks

With all the growing that happens during puberty, it's not surprising that some boys get stretch marks on their skin. On fair-skinned boys, they appear as purplish marks on the skin. In dark-skinned boys they may be lighter than the surrounding skin. Stretch marks usually fade with time.

Nearsightedness

Myopia is the medical term for near-sightedness. If you can see things up close just fine, but you have trouble seeing things at a distance, you may have myopia.

Myopia often gets worse during puberty and many new cases develop during this time.

Adam's Apple

Male hormones also cause changes in the angle of the portion of thyroid cartilage known as the Adam's Apple. As a result, this part of the throat may become more noticeable.

Overwhelmed?

Have we overwhelmed you with puberty bummers? We didn't mean to. The changes described on this page don't happen to everyone. We just wanted to make sure that if any of them do happen to you, you'll know what's going on and that it's perfectly normal.

Growing Up: What's in it for you?

Talking about things like B.O., zits, and other such bummers can make puberty sound like the pits. So, we'd like you to remind yourself of all of the good things about growing up. Use the space below to make a list of good things about growing up—things you can do now that you're not a "kid" anymore or that you'll be able to do once you're older. Then turn the page and see how your answers compare to other boys and girls your age.

_____

_____

_____

_____

_____

_____

_____

If You Could...

Answer the following questions:

If you could be any age, what age would you be? _____

If you could be anybody in the whole world, who would you be? _____

_____

If you could be anything you wanted to be, what would you choose

to be? _____

Growing Up Perks

Here are some lists from other kids your age.

★ More privileges
★ Getting my braces off
★ Getting a job
★ Getting to stay out later
★ Dating
★ Being more my own boss
★ Driving a car
★ Getting in to see R-rated movies
★ New friends

★ Having my body get stronger
★ Going to parties
★ New school
★ Having my own money
★ More respect
★ Joining the team in high school
★ More allowance
★ Making my own decisions (some-times)
★ Going to college
★ Hanging out more with my friends
★ Baby-sitting younger kids
★ Getting really good at something (karate, art)

Picture Your Future

You've found a magic lamp, rubbed it, and out pops a genie who grants you a wish for the future. Complete the picture below by drawing a wish you have for your future.

Resource Section

Bell, Ruth. *Changing Bodies, Changing Lives: A Book for Teens on Sex and Relationships*, revised edition (New York: Random House, 1988).

A fine book, representing many points of view through quotes from teenagers themselves. The section on teenage pregnancy is especially good, and the one on mental health, depression, and suicide is outstanding. The book is geared toward the 15- to 19-year-old age group, but it could be valuable for younger and older people as well.

Calderone, Mary S., M.D., and Johnson, Eric W. *The Family Book About Sexuality* (New York: HarperCollins, 1990).

Designed for the whole family, this book talks about how sexuality begins when we are only tiny babies, and how it develops through puberty and adulthood, and even into old age.

Cole, Joanna. *Asking About Sex and Growing Up* (New York: Morrow Junior Books, 1988).

This book was written for somewhat younger boys and girls, but older readers will find that it answers many of their questions about puberty and sexuality.

Madaras, Lynda and Area. *My Body, My Self for Girls* (New York: Newmarket Press, 1993).

This book is filled with exercises and activities that focus on the changes that happen to girls as they go through puberty.

Madaras, Lynda with Area. *My Feelings, My Self: Lynda Madaras' Growing Up Guide for Girls* (New York: Newmarket Press, 1993).

For preteen and teenage girls, this is a workbook/journal to help girls explore their relationships with parents and friends. It includes quizzes, exercises, and space to record personal experiences.

Madaras, Lynda, with Saavedra, Dane. *The "What's Happening to My Body?" Book for Boys* (New York: Newmarket Press, 1988).

This is the companion book to My Body, My Self for Boys in which Lynda and a teenage friend explain the body changes that take place in a boy's body during puberty. It has a lot more detailed information than we had room for in this book. If you have unanswered questions, we'd be willing to bet you'll find the answers here.

Madaras, Lynda with Area. *The "What's Happening to My Body?" Book for Girls* (New York: Newmarket Press, 1988).

This is a book that Lynda and Area wrote for girls about puberty. Needless to say, we think it's a pretty good one. Although it was written for girls, many boys and parents have read it and told us they learned a lot from it.

Planned Parenthood. *Kids Need to Know.*

This is an information kit for parents and teens that includes booklets and pamphlets on topics such as sexuality and birth control. The kit is available for $10.00 (which includes shipping and handling) from the Information and Education Department, Planned Parenthood, 1316 Third Street Promenade, Suite B5, Santa Monica, California, 90401.

Siegal, Peggy. *Changes In You* (Richmond, Virginia: Family Life Education Associates, 1991).

There are actually two books with the same title—one for boys and one for girls. These books are short and concise (less than 50 pages), but they fully explain the changes of puberty.

Parenting and Childcare Books
from Newmarket Press

Baby Massage
Parent-Child Bonding Through Touching
Amelia D. Auckett; Introduction by Dr. Tiffany Field

A fully-illustrated, practical, time-tested approach to the ancient art of baby massage. Topics include bonding and body contact; baby massage as an alternative to drugs, healing the effects of birth trauma; and massage as an expression of love. Includes 34 photographs and drawings, a bibliography, and an index. (128 pages; 5 1/2" x 8 1/4"; paperback)

How Do We Tell the Children?
A Step-by-Step Guide for Helping Children Two to Teen Cope When Someone Dies—Updated Edition
Dan Schaefer and Christine Lyons; Foreword by David Peretz, M.D.

This invaluable book provides straightforward language to help parents explain death to children from age two through teens. It includes insights from psychologists, educators, and clergy. Special features include a 16-page crisis-intervention guide to deal with situations such as accidents, AIDS, terminal illness, and suicide. "Parents need this clear, extremely readable guide. . . highly recommended." (*Library Journal*) (192 pages; 5 1/2" x 8 1/4"; hardcover & paperback)

How to Shoot Your Kids on Home Video
Moviemaking for the Whole Family
David Hajdu

The perfect book for the video-age family and classroom from the editor of *Video Review*. Offers parents and teachers a lively, user-friendly look at making wonderful home videos. Includes eleven ready-to-shoot scripts, clear photographs, and an index. (208 pages; 7 1/4" x 9"; paperback)

In Time and With Love
Caring for the Special Needs Baby
Marilyn Segal, Ph.D.

From a psychologist and mother of a handicapped daughter, sensitive, practical advice on care for children who are physically handicapped, developmentally delayed, or constitutionally difficult. Topics include developing motor skills; learning language; developing problem-solving abilities; and interacting with siblings, family members, and friends. Includes fifty photographs, six resource guides, a bibliography, and an index. (208 pages; 7 1/4" x 9"; hardcover & paperback)

Lynda Madaras Talks to Teens About AIDS

An Essential Guide for Young People—Updated Edition

Lynda Madaras; Forewords by Linda Levin, M.D., and Constance Wofsy, M.D.

Written for parents, teachers, and young adults ages 14 through 19, this valuable book describes with honesty and sensitivity what AIDS is, why teens need to know about it, how it is transmitted, and how to stay informed about it. Includes drawings, a bibliography, and a resource guide. (128 pages; 5 1/2" x 8 1/4"; hardcover & paperback)

Mothering the New Mother

Your Postpartum Resource Companion

Sally Placksin

This all-in-one resource guide covers everything from homecare options, help for breastfeeding problems, and workplace negotiation strategies, to adjusting to full-time motherhood, postpartum depression, and hiring a doula. Each chapter is filled with practical suggestions; hands-on solutions; and an invaluable listing of the newsletters, books, hotlines, videocassettes, support groups, services, and caregivers available to the new mother. Includes checklists, planning sheets, an index, and resource guides. (352 pages; 7 1/4" x 9"; paperback)

My Body, My Self for Boys

The What's Happening to My Body? Workbook

Lynda Madaras and Area Madaras

Packed with drawings, cartoons, games, checklists, quizzes, and innovative exercises, this book encourages boys to address head on, their concerns with their body, body image, height, weight, growth, hair, voice changes, reproductive organs, sexuality, emotional problems of puberty, diet and health.—Madaras; Winners of three *American Library Association* "Best Books of the Year" Awards. (112 pages; 7 1/4" x 9"; paperback)

My Body, My Self for Girls

The What's Happening to My Body? Workbook

Lynda Madaras and Area Madaras

The companion book to *The What's Happening to My Body? Book for Girls*, this workbook/diary encourages girls ages 9 to 15 to explore their feelings about their changing bodies. Everything affected by the onset of puberty is covered, from body image, pimples, and cramps, to first periods, first bras, and first impressions. Includes quizzes, checklists, exercises, and illustrations. (128 pages; 7 1/4" x 9"; paperback)

My Feelings, My Self
Lynda Madaras' Growing-Up Guide for Girls
Lynda Madaras with Area Madaras

For preteens and teens, a workbook/journal to help girls explore their changing relationships with parents and friends; complete with quizzes, exercises, letters, and space to record personal experiences. Includes drawings and a bibliography. (160 pages; 7 1/4" x 9"; paperback)

Raising Your Jewish/Christian Child
How Interfaith Parents Can Give Children the Best of Both Their Heritages
Lee F. Gruzen, Forewords by Rabbi Lavey Derby and the Reverend Canon Joel A. Gibson

This pioneering guide details how people have found their own paths in Jewish/Christian marriages, and how they have given their children a solid foundation to seek their own identity. Includes a bibliography and an index. (288 pages; 5 5/16" x 8"; paperback)

The Ready-to-Read, Ready-to-Count Handbook
How to Best Prepare Your Child for School—A Parent's Guide
Teresa Savage

A step-by-step guide that shows how to teach preschoolers basic phonics and numbers. Over 60 phonetic learning exercises, 35 games, homemade flashcards, 24 assignments, and a series of cartoons encourage a tension-free, fun-filled environment while your child develops skills in motor ability, logic, listening, and comprehension. Includes a bibliography, an index, and reference lists. (272 pages; 5 5/16" x 8"; paperback)

Saying No Is Not Enough
Raising Children Who Make Wise Decisions About Drugs and Alcohol
Robert Schwebel, Ph.D.; Introduction by Benjamin Spock, M.D.

Widely praised as the first book to present a complete program on how to empower children to defend themselves against drugs, this step-by-step guide shows parents and counselors how to help kids develop the self-confidence and skills necessary to make life-protecting decisions about drugs and alcohol. "Wise and wondrously specific...a solid parental manual." (*Kirkus Reviews*) Includes a bibliography and an index. (256 pages; 5 5/16" x 8"; hardcover & paperback)

The Totally Awesome Money Book for Kids (and Their Parents)
Adriane G. Berg and Arthur Berg Bochner

For young readers from ten to seventeen, this fun, fact-filled guide uses quizzes, games, riddles, stories, and drawings to teach the basics of saving, investing, borrowing, working, taxes, and more. Includes illustrations, a bibliography and a glossary. An *American Library Association* "Best Book of the Year" finalist.(160 pages; 5 5/16" x 8"; hardcover & paperback)

The Totally Awesome Business Book for Kids (and Their Parents)
Adriane G. Berg and Arthur Berg Bochner

Everything kids need to know about business with special attention to jobs that help the environment. Introduces vital business skills such as research, telephoning, negotiating, complaining when appropriate, making contracts, filing, and record keeping. Includes illustrations, a bibliography and a glossary. (160 pages; 5 5/16" x 8"; paperback)

The What's Happening to My Body? Book for Boys
A Growing Up Guide for Parents and Sons—New Edition
Lynda Madaras with Dane Saavedra

Written with candor, humor, and clarity, here is much-needed, but hard-to-find information on the special problems boys face during puberty. It includes chapters on the body's changing size and shape, hair, perspiration, pimples, and voice changes; the reproductive organs; sexuality; female puberty; and more. "Down-to-earth, conversational treatment of a topic that remains taboo in many families." (*The Washington Post*) Includes drawings, charts, diagrams, a bibliography, and an index. (288 pages; 5 1/2" x 8 1/4"; hardcover & paperback)

The What's Happening to My Body? Book for Girls
A Growing Up Guide for Parents and Daughters—New Edition
Lynda Madaras with Area Madaras

Selected as a "Best Book for Young Adults" by the *American Library Association*, this bestselling book provides explains what takes place in a girl's body as she grows up. Includes chapters on the body's changing size and shape; the reproductive organs; menstruation; male puberty; and much more. Includes drawings, charts, diagrams, a bibliography, and an index. (304 pages; 5 1/2" x 8 1/4"; hardcover & paperback)

Your Child at Play: Birth to One Year
Discovering the Senses and Learning About the World
Marilyn Segal, Ph.D.

Focuses on the subtle developmental changes that take place in each of the first twelve months of life and features over 400 activities that parent and child can enjoy together during day-to-day routines. "Insightful, warm, and practical...expert knowledge that's a must for every parent." (T. Berry Brazelton, M.D.) Includes more than 250 photographs and a bibliography. (288 pages; 7 1/4" x 9"; hardcover & paperback)

Your Child at Play: One to Two Years
Exploring, Daily Living, Learning, and Making Friends
Marilyn Segal, Ph.D., and Don Adcock, Ph.D.

Hundreds of suggestions for creative play and for coping with everyday life with a toddler, including situations such as going out in public, toilet training, and sibling rivalry. "An excellent guide to the hows, whys, and what-to-dos of play." (*Publishers Weekly*) Includes more than 300 photographs, a bibliography, and an index. (224 pages; 7 1/4" x 9"; hardcover & paperback)

Your Child at Play: Two to Three Years
Growing Up, Language, and the Imagination
Marilyn Segal, Ph.D., and Don Adcock, Ph.D.

Provides vivid descriptions of how two-year-olds see themselves, learn language, play imaginatively, get along with others, make friends, and explore what's around them. It give specific advice on routine problems and concerns common to this age group. Includes more than 175 photographs, a bibliography, and an index. (208 pages; 7 1/4" x 9"; hardcover & paperback)

Your Child at Play: Three to Five Years
Conversation, Creativity, and Learning Letters, Words, and Numbers
Marilyn Segal, Ph.D., and Don Adcock, Ph.D.

Hundreds of practical ideas for exploring the world of the preschooler, with sections devoted to conversation, creative play, learning letters and numbers, and making friends. Includes more than 100 photographs, a bibliography, and an index. (224 pages; 7 1/4" x 9"; hardcover & paperback)

Ask for these titles at your local bookstore or use this coupon and enclose a check or money order payable to: **Newmarket Press**, 18 E. 48th St., NY, NY 10017.

Baby Massage
____ $10.00 pb (1-55704-022-2)
How Do We Tell the Children?
____ $18.95 hc (1-55704-189-X)
____ $10.95 pb 1-55704-181-4)
How to Shoot Your Kids on Home Video
____ $10.95 pb (1-55704-013-3)
In Time and With Love
____ $21.95 hc (0-937858-95-1)
____ $12.95 pb (0-937858-96-X)
Lynda Madaras Talks to Teens About AIDS
____ $16.95 hc (1-55704-188-1)
____ $7.95 pb (1-55704-180-6)
Mothering the New Mother
____ $15.95 pb (1-55704-178-4)
My Body, My Self for Boys
____ $11.95 pb (1-55704-230-6)
My Body, My Self for Girls
____ $11.95 pb (1-55704-150-4)
My Feelings, My Self
____ $9.95 pb (1-55704-157-1)
Raising Your Jewish/Christian Child
____ $10.95 pb (1-55704-059-1)
The Ready-to-Read,
Ready-to-Count Handbook
____ $11.95 pb (1-55704-093-1)
Saying No Is Not Enough
____ $18.95 hc (1-55704-041-9)
____ $10.95 pb (1-55704-078-8)

The Totally Awesome Business Book
for Kids (and Their Parents)
____ $10.95 pb (1-55704-226-8)
The Totally Awesome Money Book
for Kids (and Their Parents)
____ $18.95 hc (1-55704-183-0)
____ $10.95 pb (1-55704-176-8)
The What's Happening to My Body?
Book for Boys
____ $18.95 hc (1-55704-002-8)
____ $11.95 pb (0-937858-99-4)
The What's Happening to My Body?
Book for Girls
____ $18.95 hc (1-55704-001-X)
____ $11.95 pb (0-937858-98-6)
Your Child at Play: Birth to One Year
____ $21.95 hc (0-937858-50-1)
____ $12.00 pb (0-937858-51-X)
Your Child at Play: One to Two Years
____ $21.95 hc (0-937858-52-8)
____ $12.00 pb (0-937858-53-6)
Your Child at Play: Two to Three Years
____ $21.95 hc (0-937858-54-4)
____ $10.95 pb (0-937858-55-2)
Your Child at Play: Three to Five Years
____ $21.95 hc (0-937858-72-2)
____ $12.00 pb (0-937858-73-0)

For postage and handling, please add $2.50 for the first book, plus $1.00 for each additional book. For orders of five or more copies, please add 5% for shipping and handling. Prices and availability are subject to change.

I enclose a check or money order payable to **Newmarket Press** in the amount of _____

Name_____

Address_____

City/State/Zip_____

For discounts on orders of five or more copies, contact Newmarket Press, Special Sales Department, 18 East 48th Street, NY, NY 10017; Tel.: 212-832-3575 or 800-669-3903; Fax: 212-832-3629.

chld2bob.QXD